CELEBRATING

Kosher

WITH THE BUTCHER'S WIFE

The book is dedicated with absolute love to my Butcher, Iani.
And our precious children, Boruch, Rochi, Darren, Ryan and Eden,
and grandchildren, Zahara and Leah.

SHARON LURIE

ACKNOWLEDGEMENTS

There's an old Yiddish saying my father (OBM) always used: '*Mach zich nisht visendik*,' which we understood as, 'Make like you don't know!' Like if you're driving and a policeman stops you for speeding, you say 'What? They have speed limits here?'

To my very special editor, Bronwen Leak, who really bore the brunt of this statement! 'What, there's a deadline for this book?' Bronwen, thank you for allowing me to continue writing until the 'examiner forced me to put down my pen'!

To Beverley Dodd, my designer, who had to have a couple of *le chaims* before she could appreciate where this saying comes from – 'You telling me I can't use the same cover as last time?'

Thank you to Linda de Villiers, my publisher, who allowed me to think that I could 'make like I didn't know', but knew better!

To Rebbetzin Batya Kurtstag who, when I really didn't know, was there to help and encourage me with, 'but you knew that anyway!'

To my food stylist, Lyn Woodward, your respect for our kosher laws is so appreciated. No, we don't wash all our Villeroy and Boch under a cold running tap outside, only yours!

To my creative stylist, Kari of Kari's Flowers, how lucky I was to have you work with me on my book. Your talent, creativity, attention to detail and dedication made you a dream to work with.

A very special thank you to Ken Rayner who was so generous in allowing us to photograph the chapter openers at his magnificent function venue, Shepstone Gardens. Not only is the location stunning, but Ken, his family and his assistant, Marielle Evans, couldn't have made our experience any more pleasurable.

To all my special friends who were always there for me, even when you called and I said, 'Can't talk, deadlines, call you back', and never did!

To my mother, Jill, and my mother-in-law, Roch, may all of the recipes from our past with some updated twists from the present PG keep our families united in the future.

We have a *minhag* (tradition) in our family and that is that we don't like to thank our immediate family publicly. Nobody really wants to hear how wonderful parents, brothers, sisters and children are! It's boring! We tell each other privately. Even better, we write beautiful letters where we open our hearts and bawl our eyes out! HOWEVER, I have to thank one very, very special person and that is Michael. After looking through this book, you'll realise why. Simply because he is the photographer! He is a genius, a perfectionist and he's my little brother!

SHARON LURIE

The author and publisher would like to thank the following for the loan of props for the shoot: Décor Mechanics, Fancy Affairs, House of Judaica, Imagine Nation, La Basse-cour, Liebermann Pottery & Tableware, Lucky Fish, MG Design Box, Party Creations, Party Design, Tanya Joselowsky of Pop Balloons and The Kollel Bookshop.

Published in 2011 by Struik Lifestyle
(an imprint of Random House Struik (Pty) Ltd)
Company Reg. No. 1966/003153/07
80 McKenzie Street, Cape Town 8001
PO Box 1144, Cape Town, 8000, South Africa

Reproduction: Hirt & Carter Cape (Pty) Ltd
Printing and binding: Tien Wah Press (Pte) Ltd, Singapore

Copyright © in published edition:
Random House Struik (Pty) Ltd 2011
Copyright © in text: Sharon Lurie 2011
Copyright © in photographs: Michael Smith 2011

PUBLISHER: Linda de Villiers
MANAGING EDITOR: Cecilia Barfield
EDITOR AND INDEXER: Bronwen Leak
DESIGNER: Beverley Dodd
PHOTOGRAPHER: the redhead's studio – Michael Smith
FOOD STYLISTS: Lyn Woodward and Kari Berkowitz
PROOFREADER: Tessa Kennedy

ISBN 978-1-77007-866-6

CONTENTS

INTRODUCTION

This book is all about celebrating! Celebrating rest on Shabbat, celebrating freedom from slavery on Pesach, celebrating our jubilance in receiving the Torah on Shavuot, celebrating a new year on Rosh Hashanah, celebrating our confidence in Hashem as we move from Yom Kippur into Sukkot, celebrating our never-ending dedication to the Torah on Simchat Torah, celebrating the miracles of both Chanukkah and Purim and, all the while, celebrating life itself.

For me, each *chag* (holiday) possesses its own vibrancy and colour, and I hope to portray this happiness and brightness through the use of colour in this book. Each festival brings its own unique customs and traditions with regards to food and this certainly doesn't mean 'old-fashioned' foods. Who would have thought we would ever eat Thai fishcakes (page 54) on Pesach, put BBQ sauces into cholent (page 41) and serve chopped liver in choux pastry (page 20)? With the ever-increasing variety of new kosher products available, twists on traditional foods have enabled us to follow food trends, while keeping within tradition.

Although a recipe may be placed under a particular holiday in this book, it doesn't mean it's restricted to that holiday. Chicken soup (page 23) with kneidlach (page 58) goes down very well all year round, not only on Pesach. And brisket recipes aren't just for Rosh Hashanah or Pesach. If you enjoy theme evenings, have a deli evening during Sukkot and serve hot beef on rye. Or host an Italian evening and serve lasagne (page 72) and pizzas (page 190). Or why not try an Indian evening with a delicious bunny chow (page 171)? For this reason, I have given Sukkot and Chanukkah more recipes, as they're both eight-day celebrations. Purim is only one day, hence its chapter is a little 'thinner'.

Celebrating a *chag* doesn't just 'happen' on the day. It's all about the build-up! For me, getting into the Shabbat and Yomtov mood means getting into the kitchen! That's when I start feeling it in the air, or rather in my back and feet! My husband always says I'm a bit OTT (over the top) when it comes to preparing for Shabbat and Yomtov, but I like to do a 'dish a day'. Making the ice creams, soups and freeze-able dishes in advance makes things so much easier, as there are always last-minute things to do, such as taking your daughter shopping because she's 'got nothing to wear'! As for my table? Let's just say that by Wednesday it's already laid for Shabbat! Maybe I'm a bit meshuga, but I console myself with these wise words from Rebbetzin Mashi Lipskar: 'One should have Shabbat in mind every day of the week!'

For a relaxed Shabbat and laid-back Yomtov, I like to use the Three 'P' Principle: Plan, Prepare and Place. If you've planned and prepared your food, then all that's left to do is place it on the dining room table. The dining room table, therefore, plays a very important role in our lives: it is a place to gather and draw in family and friends, where your being hospi**table** makes them feel comfor**table**, while sharing food so delec**table** that the moments become unforget**table**!

Shabbat and the *Chagim* are there for each and every one of us to enjoy with our families and friends and don't need to be left for the 'frum side of the family' to take care of.

They say that the sense of smell is the most powerful reminder of our past. I hope the aromas created in your kitchen from these recipes become the most powerful reminders of our future.

OVEN TEMPERATURES

CELSIUS (C)	FAHRENHEIT (F)	GAS MARK
100 °C	200 °F	¼
110 °C	225 °F	¼
120 °C	250 °F	½
140 °C	275 °F	1
150 °C	300 °F	2
160 °C	325 °F	3
180 °C	350 °F	4
190 °C	375 °F	5
200 °C	400 °F	6
220 °C	425 °F	7
230 °C	450 °F	8
240 °C	475 °F	9

CONVERSION TABLE

METRIC	US CUPS	IMPERIAL
5 ml	1 tsp	1 tsp
15 ml	1 Tbsp	1 Tbsp
60 ml	4 Tbsp (¼ cup)	2 fl oz
80 ml	⅓ cup	2¾ fl oz
125 ml	½ cup	4½ fl oz
160 ml	⅔ cup	5½ fl oz
200 ml	¾ cup	7 fl oz
250 ml	1 cup	9 fl oz

Boruch

SHABBAT

שבת

SHABBAT

Ask some of the finest life coaches and time-management consultants what they include in their 10-step programme to a successful and happy life and I guarantee you after 'setting goals' comes 'take time out for yourself'.

This same commandment was given to us thousands of years ago in G-d's own blueprint for a successful life: the Torah, where He advocates one day a week of total rest, that being Shabbat.

Since all cooking must have stopped by the time Shabbat begins, preparations are quite hectic, fast paced and *lebbedik* (lively), for want of a better word. But once those candles are lit, it's as if we close our eyes to everything running on fast-forward and open them to a serene world of slow motion.

Shabbat is the highlight of my week, mainly because the whole family is together on Friday night. It's a time to catch up on all the week's news and to just laugh. For me, the smell of challah (kitke) baking on a Friday afternoon almost says it all. It leaves the whole house smelling of Shabbat. This, together with the white tablecloth, the silverware, wine, fresh flowers and delicious food, makes Shabbat the special weekly meal it should be. What a perfect way to end the week!

CHOPPPED HERRING made with love and caring

Sushi, shmushi! Ceviche, deep sea! If it's raw fish you fancy, then there's always the traditional chopped herring.

6 Bismark herrings (12 sides)	1 Tbsp sugar (or to taste)
4 large Granny Smith apples, peeled, cored and quartered	pinch of ground cinnamon
	pinch of salt
7 hard-boiled eggs	2 Tbsp white vinegar
1 onion, peeled and chopped	

1. Mince the herrings, apples, 6 of the eggs and the onion.
2. Mix in the sugar, cinnamon, salt and vinegar.
3. If you like, you can add matzo meal, finger biscuits or pareve crackers. Sometimes the apples are really juicy. If you find the mixture is a little too loose, place it in a sieve and drain off a little of the excess liquid or mince some crackers into it to bind the herring a little more.
4. Spoon onto a serving platter, grate the remaining egg and sprinkle it on top of the herring.
5. Serve with Aunty Min's kichel (see page 11).

SERVES 12

HUNGARIAN CUCUMBER salad

This is one of those salads that everybody loves, nobody wants to share and anybody can make. But guess who that somebody is going to be?

2 English cucumbers, peeled and thinly sliced (I use a mandolin slicer)
2 tsp salt
2 red onions, peeled and sliced into thin rounds

SALAD DRESSING
½ cup white vinegar
½ cup water
2 tsp sugar
½ tsp salt and ¼ tsp pepper
¼ tsp paprika
2 cloves garlic, crushed

1. Place the cucumber slices in a colander and sprinkle over the salt. Mix well. Allow to stand for 30 minutes and then squeeze out the juices by placing a plate on top of the cucumber and gently pushing the juice out.
2. Combine the cucumber and onion in a salad bowl.
3. Combine the dressing ingredients in a jar and shake well. Pour the dressing over the salad and serve immediately.

SERVES 6–8

ITALIAN TOMATO salad

This is a lovely fresh accompaniment to fish or meat. If I'm doing an Italian theme for Sukkot, I make this salad as well. A little twist is to fry some cubed stale bread in a little oil and garlic (not deep-fried like croutons) and toss them into the salad about 20 minutes before serving. You could add some olives at this point too.

6 large tomatoes (not too red)
1 large red onion, peeled and chopped
¼ cup roughly chopped fresh basil
¼ cup chopped fresh parsley

SALAD DRESSING
¼ cup red wine vinegar
½ cup oil
¼ cup brown treacle sugar
½ tsp prepared mild mustard
1 tsp salt and ¼ tsp pepper
2 cloves garlic, crushed

1. Place the tomatoes in a bowl and pour boiling water over them, ensuring that they are completely immersed. You can leave the skins on if you are in a hurry. Allow to stand for 3–4 minutes and then remove the skins. If the skin doesn't slip off (this is the problem when the tomatoes aren't very red), then pour off the water and cover them again in boiling water. Once peeled, refrigerate the tomatoes for 1 hour.
2. Cut the cooled tomatoes in half and, using your fingers, scoop out the pips. Chop the tomatoes into small pieces.
3. Combine the chopped tomatoes, onion, basil and parsley in a salad bowl.
4. Combine the salad dressing ingredients in a jar and shake well. Pour over the salad and chill before serving.

SERVES 8

AUNTY MIN'S kichel

My mother-in-law and her sister, Minnie Wesek, (AKA 'the koeksisters') always got together just before Yomtov to cook. The kichel, perogen, herring and fish that they pumped out of that kitchen were amazing. Then Aunty Min emigrated, but TG she left her recipes and sister behind!

I have to tell you a quick story. It was a Thursday afternoon and I decided I was going to try, for the first time ever, to make Aunty Min's kichel for Shabbat. On the Thursday night, my son Darren had some friends over for a game of cards. While walking past, I casually heard him say, 'Oh ja, they're great – nobody makes kichel like my mom!' What? I would have thought biltong and droëwors would have gone down better at a card game, certainly not dry kichel! It seemed that the kichel won hands down as there was not one left! Did I make another batch for Shabbat? No, I just wallowed in self-pride as he told the family: 'Trust me, they were good.'

3 eggs, separated
3 Tbsp sugar
3 Tbsp oil
2 cups cake flour
3 tsp baking powder
little extra oil
sugar to sprinkle on top

1. Preheat the oven to 180 °C.
2. In a large bowl, beat the egg yolks with the sugar and oil.
3. In a separate bowl, beat the egg whites until firm, and then very gently fold into the egg-yolk mixture.
4. Sift half of the flour over the egg mixture and fold in with a large spoon.
5. Once incorporated, sift the other half of the flour with the baking powder and fold this in too.
6. Once you have formed a nice dough, you can either refrigerate it for about half an hour or start rolling it out immediately.
7. Roll out about a third of the dough as thinly as possible on a lightly floured surface.
8. Cut into squares, diamonds or circles and place onto a lightly oiled baking tray. Alternatively, you can bake them on a lightly oiled wire rack to get that authentic crisscross pattern.
9. Repeat until all the dough is used up.
10. Brush with a little oil and sprinkle with sugar.
11. Bake for 8–10 minutes until very lightly browned.

MAKES ABOUT 40 (ASK DARREN – HE ATE THEM ALL!)

'SOME LIKE IT HOT' salmon salad

It was one of those days when a quiet Shabbat lunch for four turned into a lebbedikke *Shabbat lunch for 14. In a flash, we created this salad, which has now become a firm family favourite!*

500 g smoked salmon bits

2 red onions, peeled and sliced

250 g fresh asparagus, chopped

handful of fresh flat-leaf parsley, roughly chopped

2 Tbsp schug (hot chilli mix – made by most kosher delis) or 1 heaped tsp homemade chilli sauce
   (see page 25)

2 Tbsp capers (optional)

2 cups Italian salad dressing (I use Knorr as the catering size is kosher)

1. Mix all the ingredients in a salad bowl and serve.
2. As it is quite hot and spicy, make sure you have some extra challah around!

SERVES 8–10

talking about CHALLAH ...

Here's the quickest challah recipe in town!

PLACE THE FOLLOWING, IN THE SAME ORDER, INTO A MIXMASTER WITH A DOUGH HOOK:

1 cup warm water

8 cups all-purpose flour

2 x 10 g sachets rapid-rising yeast

4 tsp salt

¾ cup sugar

¾ cup oil

2 eggs

2 cups warm water

1. With your Mixmaster on its lowest speed, blend until all of the ingredients are combined, then increase the speed a little and continue kneading until the mixture forms a nice, well-blended ball of dough. You may need to add a little more water if the dough is too firm or a little more flour if the dough is still sticking to the sides of the bowl.
2. Allow the dough to rise for 1–2 hours until doubled in size, punch down and divide into 4 equal portions. Shape each into a loaf or plait as desired and place on a baking tray. Allow to rise again until doubled in size and then paint with egg wash (1 egg yolk mixed with 2 Tbsp water).
3. Preheat the oven to 180 °C and bake the challah for 30–35 minutes until golden brown. So easy, so simple and ever so fulfilling!

MAKES 4 MEDIUM-SIZED CHALLAH

'Some like it hot' salmon salad

smoked steak SUSHI CAKE

What do you do if your family believes that a meal is not complete without meat? This was created for my son Ryan who loves sushi, but won't eat fish. As most of the starters in our home are meat, I like to serve this together with a platter of beef carpaccio (see next page). The length of the ingredient list doesn't make the recipe lengthier and harder, sometimes just a little tastier!

2 cups raw sushi rice
¼ cup Manischewitz® Creamy
Horseradish Sauce – Wasabi
1¼ cups mayonnaise
500 g smoked steak, finely sliced
1½ cups grated carrot
1 large red pepper, deseeded and cut
into matchstick-size strips
2 cups finely shredded Chinese
cabbage or iceberg lettuce
1 x 340 g can whole kernel
corn, drained
½ cup chopped spring onions
1 English cucumber, cut into
matchstick-size strips
1 x 230 g can water chestnuts, drained
and finely sliced (I use Sunkist)

2 avocados
sesame seeds for sprinkling
1 pkt potato sticks (available
at Woolworths)
100 g cashew nuts, roughly crushed

DRESSING (served separately)
½ cup oil
½ cup brown sugar
¼ cup red wine vinegar
¼ cup soy sauce
¼ tsp garlic powder
¼ tsp ground ginger
1 tsp Manischewitz® Creamy Horseradish
Sauce – Wasabi
freshly ground black pepper to taste

1. Cook the raw sushi rice as per the packet instructions and allow to cool.
2. In a bowl, mix the horseradish sauce with the mayonnaise. This will be referred to as 'the sauce' from here on out.
3. Firmly press 1 cup of the cooked sushi rice (about 1 cm) into the base of a greased 22–24 cm springform tin.
4. Spread ½ cup of the sauce over the entire layer of rice.
5. Top this with half of the steak, followed by the grated carrot, then the red pepper and finally the Chinese cabbage or iceberg lettuce.
6. Add another layer of sushi rice and spread ½ cup of the sauce over it.
7. Top this with the corn, followed by the spring onions, the cucumber, the chestnuts and finally the remaining steak.
8. Cover with a final layer of sushi rice. Place a piece of wax wrap on top of the rice and gently press down on the cake to compress it.
9. Refrigerate for up to a day. Just before serving, remove the cake from the tin, plate it and cover with the remaining sauce.
10. Slice the avocados into wedges and arrange them on top of the cake.
11. Sprinkle with sesame seeds and pile the potato sticks and cashew nuts on top.
12. To make the dressing, place all of the ingredients into a bottle with a lid, close tightly and shake well.
13. Allow to stand for a bit and shake up again just before serving with the cake.

SERVES 8–10

BEEF CARPACCIO with tomato vinaigrette

This is one of those dishes that took me about five years to appreciate. But when I finally did, this was the recipe that did it for me.

	TOMATO VINAIGRETTE
little oil for frying and drizzling	250 g baby tomatoes, quartered
1 kg Scotch fillet	1 small red onion, peeled and finely grated
2 Tbsp cracked black peppercorns	2 Tbsp honey
1 bunch of fresh coriander or basil	1 Tbsp red wine vinegar
(about 50 g), finely chopped or	1 Tbsp lemon juice
blitzed in a food processor	½ cup oil

1. Heat a large frying pan with a little oil and evenly sear the meat for 10–15 minutes or until dark brown. Rotate the meat slowly to ensure that the whole surface gets browned. At this point you're not trying to cook the meat, you are only searing the outside as I feel it makes it a little more appetising; some people don't even sear it – they leave it raw. Allow to cool.
2. Drizzle a little oil on a large piece of foil and spread the cracked peppercorns and coriander or basil in the centre.
3. Roll the fillet in the mixture so that it is completely covered. Wrap it in the foil and tightly secure the ends. Refrigerate for 30 minutes before transferring to the freezer. Freeze for 4–5 hours.
4. Make the tomato vinaigrette by combining all the ingredients in a bowl and store in the fridge until needed.
5. Remove the meat from the freezer and allow to stand at room temperature for about 45 minutes, depending on the temperature outside.
6. If you have a cold-meat slicer or an electric bread slicer, slice the fillet paper-thin. Otherwise, using a very sharp carving knife, slice the fillet as thinly as possible. Lay the slices on a platter, cover and refrigerate. This should be done on Friday afternoon and left in the fridge for lunch the next day.
7. Just before serving, drizzle the tomato vinaigrette around the edges of the platter. Do not put it directly on the meat, as the vinegar will 'cook' it.

SERVES 8–10

CARIBBEAN CHICKEN SALAD
with toasted coconut and sweet-chilli dressing

It's crispy, it's cool, it's crunchy and it's Caribbean! The toasted coconut gives it a totally different tropical-island flavour.
I couldn't throw in the palm trees and rum, but there's nothing to stop you from making your own daiquiris!

½ cup finely shredded coconut (you have to put this in even if you don't like coconut!)
4 thick chicken schnitzels
1 tsp Cajun spice
2 Tbsp cornflour
oil for frying
500 g mixed salad leaves
2 avocados, peeled and sliced
1 mango, peeled and sliced
1 small pineapple; slice half into matchstick-size pieces and keep the other half for the salad dressing
1 red onion, peeled and finely sliced

1 red pepper, deseeded and finely shredded
½ cup cashew nuts, roasted

SALAD DRESSING
½ small pineapple, chunked (saved from the salad)
⅓ cup sweet chilli sauce
¼ cup apple cider vinegar
juice of 2 small limes or ½ lemon
2 Tbsp honey
⅓ cup sugar
1 tsp mustard powder
1 cup oil

1. Preheat the oven to 180 °C.
2. Place the shredded coconut on a baking tray and bake in the oven until golden brown. Keep moving it around with a spatula as it browns very quickly. Set aside to cool.
3. Cut each chicken schnitzel into 4 pieces and place them in a Ziploc™ bag. Add the Cajun spice and cornflour and shake the bag until each piece is evenly coated.
4. Heat the oil in a frying pan (about 1 cm up the side) and fry the chicken pieces until golden brown all over. Refrigerate when cool.
5. Just before serving, arrange the salad leaves on a salad platter and scatter over the avocados, mango, pineapple pieces, onion and pepper.
6. Finally, top with the chicken pieces.
7. Make the salad dressing by blending all the ingredients together in a food processor until smooth.
8. Drizzle over the salad, then sprinkle over the roasted cashew nuts and toasted coconut.

SERVES 6

choux pastry CHOPPED LIVER PUFFS

I have gone choux pastry crazy! And all because of a demonstration I attended in New York by David Kolotkin, Executive Chef of The Prime Grill in New York. Please don't skip this one saying, 'Oy! Too patshkedik*!' This will give your dinner the WOW factor!*

1 cup water
4 Tbsp non-dairy margarine
½ tsp salt
1 cup cake flour
4 large eggs, lightly beaten

FILLING
chopped liver (see page 58)

1. Preheat the oven to 180 °C.
2. Bring the water and margarine to the boil in a large saucepan on the stove.
3. Once the margarine has melted, remove from the heat.
4. Add the flour, all at once, and stir very fast – it should form a ball.
5. Add the eggs gradually, ensuring that they are well incorporated into the pastry.
6. Place the pastry in a piping bag and pipe long finger-length rows of pastry onto a baking tray. If you prefer, you can spoon tablespoons of the pastry onto the baking tray and bake them in a round shape.
7. Bake for about 20 minutes, then switch off the oven and leave them in for a further 20 minutes.
8. In the meantime, make up a batch of the chopped liver.
9. Blend it in a food processor to make it a little smoother, like pâté.
10. Cut off the top third of the choux pastry puffs and spoon in the liver pâté with a teaspoon. Gently replace the lids after filling.
11. Fill the pastry puffs as close to Shabbat as possible, as you don't want the choux pastry to go too soft.

Other fillings to consider:
bolognese mince
finely chopped chicken à la king

MAKES ABOUT 20 (IF YOU DON'T USE THEM ALL, FREEZE OR STORE THE UNFILLED PUFFS IN AN AIRTIGHT CONTAINER AND CRISP UP IN THE OVEN WHEN READY TO USE.)

BELLA'S SPEEDY bean soup

Reading through my mother-in-law's recipe book was truly an adventure. Newspaper cutouts were taped down to yellow-stained pages along with handwritten recipes offering some of the most delicious memories. There were recipes written on Kalooki scoring pads, the backs of outdated calendar pages and hotel letterheads, all held in place by the stringy remains of what was once a strongly bound hardcover book.

This is late Aunty Bella's recipe, which is so delicious nobody believes it takes less than an hour from start to finish! As a quick and easy winter warmer, it's wonderful!

little oil for frying
2 onions, peeled and chopped
6 celery sticks, chopped
1 bunch of fresh parsley, chopped
1 cup grated carrot
4 x 410 g cans butter beans
2 cups cold water
3 cloves garlic, crushed
3 level Tbsp cake flour
5 cups chicken stock
salt and pepper to taste

1. Heat the oil in a large soup pot and fry the onions, celery, parsley and carrot for about 10 minutes until soft.
2. Meanwhile, mash 3 of the cans of butter beans with the cold water in a bowl and set aside.
3. Add the garlic to the pot and give it a good stir.
4. Remove from the heat and add the flour. Mix well.
5. Add the stock and mashed bean mixture.
6. Season with salt and pepper, return to the heat and simmer for 30–40 minutes. Add the last can of whole butter beans and stir well.

SERVES 8

good old-fashioned CHICKEN SOUP

There are hundreds of ways to make chicken soup
And it doesn't boil down to a person's age group;
It's something we carry through every generation
Together with kneidlach, it's a healthy combination;
Most serve it on Shabbat and Yomtov too
We eat it all week 'cause it's so good for you!

1 whole chicken
2 large onions, peeled and quartered
6 celery sticks, roughly chopped
6 large carrots, peeled and chunked
5 litres water
2 chicken carcasses
some chicken necks and feet (optional – but if you're making chicken soup, go big!)
250 g pumpkin, peeled and chunked
handful of fresh parsley
1 Tbsp salt

1. Fry the chicken in a large pot (the skin has enough oil to coat the bottom) for a few minutes, until the skin turns golden brown in places. The golden brown bits are from caramelisation and give the soup a hearty taste and warm colour. If you feel that the chicken is sticking to the pan and not browning adequately, add a little oil.
2. Add the onions, celery and carrots and sauté for 1–2 minutes longer.
3. Add the water and bring to the boil.
4. Add the chicken carcasses, necks and feet (if using), pumpkin, parsley and salt and bring to the boil again.
5. Once boiling, reduce the heat and simmer for 3½–4 hours.
6. Turn off the heat and allow the soup to stand awhile and cool.
7. Strain the soup, pressing the carrots through the sieve with the back of a spoon.
8. When completely cool, refrigerate the soup for a few hours. Any fat in the soup will rise to the top and solidify, making it easier for you to remove it.
9. When ready to eat, reheat on the stove and taste the soup to see if it needs any more salt or, dare I say it, a chicken stock cube or two. I quite like adding cubes – they seem to bring it all together. However, it's still good without them.
10. I have a friend who roasts her chicken with 6 drumsticks seasoned with a little salt and pepper in the oven until golden brown. She then drains the oil off the bottom of the pan and puts the chicken and drumsticks into the soup pot with the vegetables and water. She adds 2 cups of boiling water to the pan in which the chicken was roasting, scrapes all the bits off the bottom and adds that to the soup pot as well. I've tried this once or twice and, although it is good, I sometimes don't have the time to roast then boil the chicken. A quick fry is easier.
11. Serve with kreplach (see page 214) or kneidlach (see page 58).

SERVES 12–14

3-IN-1 ROASTED BUTTERNUT SOUP with a bisl pesto – it's a bargain!

This is an 'On Special' recipe. You get three recipes for the price of one: butternut soup, chilli sauce and pesto. For those who know me, that's almost as good as less 75%. No, it's not another boring butternut soup. Yes, you must make the chilli sauce, because you can use it in at least 10 recipes in this book – see how much I'm saving you! And, it's a yes and no for the pesto sauce. You can buy it off the shelf if you have to.

1.5 kg butternut, peeled and cubed	1 tsp fresh chilli sauce (see below left)
½ cup oil	35 g fresh coriander, chopped
3 heaped Tbsp margarine (for frying veggies)	3 Tbsp vegetable stock powder
	2 litres water
3 onions, peeled and chopped	2 cups Orley Whip™ Cook 'n Crème
3 celery sticks, chopped	1 cup coconut milk
2 tsp crushed garlic	salt and pepper to taste
4 cm piece ginger, grated	

1. Preheat the oven to 190 °C.
2. Place the butternut in a roasting pan and drizzle over the oil. Roast until soft, turning every now and then. Don't let it get too dark though.
3. While the butternut is roasting, melt the margarine in a large pot and fry the onions and celery until limp, but not dark.
4. Add the garlic, ginger, chilli sauce and coriander and continue to cook for about 5 minutes.
5. Add the butternut to the pot, sprinkle over the vegetable stock powder and add the water.
6. Bring to the boil, then reduce the heat and simmer for 1–1½ hours. If you feel too much liquid has evaporated, add more water and another teaspoon of vegetable stock powder.
7. Blend the soup in a food processor until smooth.
8. Add the Orley Whip™ and coconut milk and continue to blend before straining through a sieve or colander.
9. Reheat in the pot and season with salt and pepper before serving with pesto sauce (see below right).

CHILLI SAUCE
Blend the following in a food processor until smooth:

250 g fresh small hot chillies
1 head of garlic
1 Tbsp sugar (or sweetener equivalent)
1 tsp salt
2 Tbsp vinegar
1 cup oil

Place in a glass jar with a tight-fitting lid and store upside down to prevent it from going off too soon. Every time a recipe calls for chilli or peri-peri sauce this is what you use.

CREAMY PESTO SAUCE
You can purchase a ready-made pesto and combine 3 Tbsp with ½ cup non-dairy cream or make up a pesto as follows:

35 g fresh basil leaves
50 g pine nuts
1 clove garlic
½ cup non-dairy cream
pinch of salt

Blend the ingredients in a food processor or with a hand blender and swirl a spoonful into each bowl of soup.

SERVES 12

Roasted beetfruit salad

roasted BEETFRUIT SALAD

You may get tongue-tied trying to say the name of this salad, but it's worth it!

1 kg beetroot

3 oranges, peeled and sectioned (some supermarkets have ready-peeled and sectioned oranges available)

3 Tbsp soft brown sugar dissolved in ¾ cup balsamic vinegar

2 red onions, peeled and sliced into paper-thin rings

pips of 1 pomegranate

handful of chopped fresh parsley or coriander

drizzling of olive oil

salt and coarsely ground black pepper to taste

1. Boil the beetroot (skin on) in a saucepan of water for 35–45 minutes or until soft.
2. Peel and cut the cooked beetroot in half, lay the beetroot on its flat side and slice into 3 mm-thin slices.
3. Switch on the oven griller.
4. Place the beetroot in a roasting dish, not too large as the liquid will evaporate too quickly, place the oranges on top and around the beetroot, and drizzle with the sugar and balsamic vinegar mixture.
5. Place on the middle rack of the oven and grill for 10–15 minutes until the oranges just start to turn brown here and there. The sauce should start to thicken up a bit.
6. Remove from the oven and set aside to cool.
7. When ready to serve, place the beetroot and orange, and the sauce it cooked in, into a salad bowl. Add the onion rings and sprinkle over the pomegranate pips and coriander or parsley.
8. Drizzle with olive oil and season with salt and coarsely ground black pepper and serve.

SERVES 8

red cabbage and PICKLED BEETROOT SALAD

Try this easy alternative.

1 x 780 g bottle shredded pickled beetroot, drained and juice reserved

1 small red cabbage, shredded

2 Tbsp brown sugar

1 vegetable stock cube

¼ cup sesame oil

½ cup sunflower oil

¼ cup soy sauce

2–3 Tbsp finely chopped fresh coriander

2 tsp finely grated ginger or ½ tsp ground

1. Place the drained beetroot into a bowl with the cabbage.
2. Combine the remaining ingredients with the reserved beetroot juice in the glass beetroot bottle and shake with all your might.
3. Pour this over the salad, mix well and serve. You can doll up this salad with drained mandarins, sugared nuts, dried cranberries and pomegranates. The list of options is endless, but the base good!

SERVES 8

Simple pickled Shabbat salad

simple pickled **SHABBAT SALAD**

This plain and simple, tasty salad lasts a few days and is great for Shabbat. It's good to know that there is a salad we can prepare a day or two in advance. Time is precious especially Erev Shabbat!

1 small green cabbage, finely shredded
8 red radishes, grated
2 medium carrots, peeled and grated
2 green or red peppers, deseeded and grated on large hole of grater
3 celery sticks, cut horizontally into thin slices
bunch of fresh parsley, finely chopped

SALAD DRESSING
1 cup white vinegar
3 Tbsp canola oil
5–6 cloves of garlic, crushed
½ cup sugar
1 Tbsp salt
1 tsp freshly ground black pepper

1. Place all the salad ingredients in a salad bowl.
2. Combine the dressing ingredients in a jug and mix well.
3. Pour the dressing over the salad and refrigerate for at least 6 hours before serving. Toss and serve.

SERVES YOUR SHABBAT GUESTS AND A FRIEND OR TWO!

glazed **PUMPKIN STIX**

1 kg pre-cut and peeled fresh pumpkin sticks or chunks
little olive oil for roasting
1 x 200 ml pouch Ina Paarman™ Honey and Mustard Coat & Cook Sauce
1 x 200 ml pouch Ina Paarman™ Tikka Curry Coat & Cook Sauce

1. Preheat the oven to 170 °C.
2. Cut the pumpkin sticks or chunks into 2 cm cubes.
3. Grease a roasting pan with a little olive oil.
4. Place the pumpkin in the pan and spread out evenly.
5. Evenly distribute the sauces over the pumpkin and mix well so that all the pieces are coated.
6. Bake in the oven for about 1 hour. If you find that the edges are burning, gently turn them over. However, you do want them to go a nice, dark golden colour all over.
7. If there is any left over, serve cold the next day. Combine 2–3 Tbsp chopped fresh coriander, ¼ cup mayonnaise and ¼ cup water. You may need to add a little more mayonnaise, depending on how much pumpkin is left! Pour over the pumpkin, mix gently and sprinkle with crushed peri-peri cashew nuts. Some people are nervous to try cold pumpkin – force them!

SERVES 6–8

potato **KUGEL**

Every time I think of making potato kugel, my mind goes through the following: I love it. Do we need it? If it's there, I'm going to eat it. If it's not, everyone's going to miss it. I convince myself that I use less oil in the kugel than I use in roast potatoes. Then I start craving it, needing it and, before I know it, the grater's in my hand and the kugel's in the oven!

6 large potatoes, peeled	2 tsp salt and ½ tsp pepper
2 large onions, peeled	1 Tbsp chicken stock powder
4 eggs, beaten	2 tsp baking powder
4 Tbsp cake/potato flour or matzo meal	¼ cup oil or melted schmaltz

1. Preheat the oven to 190 °C. Grate the peeled potatoes and onions either by hand or in a food processor. Alternate between grating the two, as the onions help prevent the potatoes from going brown.
2. Mix well and pour into a sieve, pressing down on the potato and onion to get rid of any excess liquid.
3. In a large bowl, combine the potatoes and onions with the eggs and mix well.
4. Add a tablespoon at a time of the flour or matzo meal and stir thoroughly.
5. Add the salt, pepper, chicken stock powder and baking powder and mix well.
6. Pour the batter into a lightly oiled roasting pan, drizzle the oil or schmaltz over the top and bake, uncovered, for about 45 minutes or until golden brown.

SERVES 12–14

roasted **BEANS**

My sister-in-law Brenda makes the tastiest, crispiest, crunchiest green beans in Dallas. And now you will be able to do just the same in South Africa. From oven to hot tray to plate, they stay just as they were made two hours before – crunchy, crispy and tasty.

olive oil spray
1 kg green beans
garlic salt to taste
freshly ground black pepper to taste

1. Preheat the oven to 240 °C. It *is* hot, but you want to roast the beans quickly.
2. Spray a baking tray with olive oil spray.
3. Top and tail the beans and place them on the baking tray.
4. Spray the beans well with olive oil spray.
5. Sprinkle over some garlic salt and black pepper.
6. Roast in the oven for about 7 minutes.
7. Remove from the oven, place in an ovenproof dish and keep warm on a hot tray.

SERVES 10–12

Potato kugel

SMITHFIELD LODGE'S stuffed farm-fresh marrow

On a recent visit to Plettenberg Bay, we stayed at a Kosher B & B for Shabbat. The daughter of the owner brought a fresh-picked large marrow from her farm which they stuffed and we ate for supper that night. It was truly delicious and tasted just like marrow! The taste brought back such fond memories of my parents' farm, Smithfield Lodge, where we went through marrow crazes, pumpkin phases and green bean stages. One of my favourites was my mom's stuffed marrow, or 'huge courgettes' as my daughter calls them.

little oil for frying
1 large onion, peeled and finely chopped
250 g mushrooms, sliced
500 g beef mince
2 Tbsp tomato paste
1 tsp sugar
½ cup cornflake crumbs
1 cup chicken stock or 1 chicken stock cube dissolved in ¾ cup water
1 cup cooked rice
salt and pepper to taste
1 large marrow, peeled, cut in half lengthways and deseeded

1. Heat the oil in a frying pan and fry the onion until golden brown.
2. Add the mushrooms and continue to fry until the liquid has evaporated.
3. Remove from the heat and set aside to cool.
4. Preheat the oven to 180 °C.
5. Place the raw mince in a bowl, add the tomato paste, sugar, cornflake crumbs, stock, rice, salt and pepper and mix until well combined.
6. Add the cooled onions and mushrooms to the mince mixture.
7. Lay the marrow halves on a large piece of lightly oiled foil. The piece of foil should be large enough to wrap around the whole marrow.
8. Divide the mince stuffing between the 2 halves, fill the halves and then sandwich them together so that they make a whole marrow.
9. Wrap the marrow in the foil and bake for 1 hour. Turn over and continue to bake for a further 45 minutes. If the marrow still feels a little hard in places, reduce the heat to 160 °C and continue to bake for another 20 minutes or until soft.
10. Slice and serve as an accompaniment to any meat dish.

SERVES 10–12

farmstyle APRICOT CHICKEN

My sister-in-law, Steph, gave my brother an orchard of fruit trees for his 40th birthday. Let's go back a step. My brother has a farm in the Magaliesberg where the mountains paint the perfect backdrop to any lazy day in a hammock. The gentle fertile slopes surrounding the farmhouse beckoned for something to be planted on them. And it was there that the fruit trees rooted, blossomed and made their home.

According to Jewish law, it is forbidden to eat the fruits of newly planted fruit trees for three years, so, as we entered the fourth, we arrived with our baskets and stripped those trees clean! We made every kind of apricot, nectarine, peach, lime and lemon dish you could ever imagine. This is what I did with my apricots.

little oil for browning
1 braai pack of chicken
8 fresh apricots or 100 g dried apricots, roughly chopped
3 Tbsp apricot jam (be my friend and I'll give you a bottle of homemade, otherwise Selwyn Segal's is great!)
⅓ cup apricot chutney (I used homemade, only because we had to get rid of the apricots before the monkeys ate them, but any shop-bought brand is just as good – maybe better!)
½ cup chicken stock
½ cup white wine (this can be replaced with another ½ cup chicken stock)
1 Tbsp finely grated fresh ginger
1 tsp curry powder
salt and pepper to taste

1. Heat the oil in a frying pan and brown the chicken pieces.
2. In the meantime, place the remaining ingredients in a saucepan and bring to the boil.
3. Preheat the oven to 170 °C.
4. Place the browned chicken pieces in a roasting pan.
5. Pour over the sauce and bake, uncovered, for 45 minutes.
6. Turn the chicken pieces over and cook for a further 35–40 minutes.

SERVES 6

SMILG, SMITH, SANTIAGO – it's still a Spanish dish!

When I think of Spain, I think of another whole side of my family I have never met who live in Murcia. They chose to use the surname Smilg (my original maiden name, which was changed to Smith upon leaving Russia). My great-uncle Sam, however, changed his name to Santiago, but just to prove we're all Smilgs at heart, I am dedicating this recipe to his family.

little olive oil for frying
1 whole chicken, cut into 10 portions
1 x 200 g box spicy Spanish flavoured rice (I use Tastic) (if you are unable to get the specified rice, then use 1 cup regular rice and crumble in 1 beef stock cube and 1 vegetable stock cube)
3 cups boiling water
500 g Russian sausages (that's just to tie in the Russian blood!)
1 large onion, peeled and finely chopped

1 tsp crushed garlic
1 red pepper, deseeded and chopped
handful of chopped fresh parsley
15–18 black olives, washed and pips removed
1 x 285 g can mushrooms
3 red Rosa tomatoes, peeled and chopped, or 1 x 410 g can chopped peeled tomatoes
1 x 65 g can tomato paste
1 tsp brown sugar
3 bay leaves
salt and pepper to taste

1. Heat the oil in a large frying pan over a high heat and fry the chicken until just brown on the outside. The chicken portions don't have to be cooked through, as they are still to be cooked in the oven. Frying simply makes them look more appetising.
2. Place the chicken portions in an ovenproof dish and cover with the rice and its flavouring and the boiling water.
3. Using the same pan, fry the Russian sausages until lightly browned and place them on top of the chicken and rice.
4. Preheat the oven to 150 °C.
5. Add a little more oil to the pan and fry the onions, garlic, red pepper, parsley and olives until soft.
6. Add the mushrooms (with their juice), tomatoes, tomato paste, sugar and bay leaves and season with salt and pepper.
7. Bring to the boil, remove from the heat and pour over the sausages and chicken.
8. Cover the dish and bake in the oven for 1½ hours. Check on it halfway through to ensure that there is enough liquid for the rice to fluff up fully. Don't mix it, because the rice may go stodgy. Just gently part the rice and see if the bottom of the dish is dry. If it is, add 1 cup warm chicken stock.

SERVES 6

'THAI ME DOWN' chicken

My brother, who won't eat any visible 'foliage', told me the only way he'd eat this dish was if I 'thaid' him down.
TG the substitution of turkey for chicken went by unnoticed too! What do they think happens to leftover turkey?
I mean really!

olive oil spray for frying	2 lemon grass sticks, outer layer removed,
1.5 kg chicken strips or chicken cut	leaves separated and finely chopped
shwarma-style	20 curry leaves
little oil for frying	1 tsp crushed fresh garlic
2 onions, peeled and	1 tsp peanut butter
roughly chopped	2 cups water
2 large leeks, roughly chopped	2 Tbsp cornflour
(remove and discard the dark	½ cup coconut milk
green heads)	juice of 1 lime
3 celery sticks, roughly chopped	1 x 410 g can creamstyle sweetcorn
1 level Tbsp finely grated	1 x 230 g can water chestnuts, drained
fresh ginger	and chopped
35 g fresh coriander,	¼ cup chopped spring onions
roughly chopped	salt and pepper to taste

1. Spray the base of a large saucepan with olive oil spray and fry the chicken in batches over a high heat until golden brown. Remove from the pan and set aside.
2. Add a little oil to the same pan and add the onions, leeks, celery, ginger, coriander, lemon grass, curry leaves, garlic and peanut butter and stir until the vegetables are soft and limp.
3. Add the water and bring to the boil. Reduce the heat and simmer for about 20 minutes. Return the chicken to the pan.
4. Dissolve the cornflour in the coconut milk and lime juice and add to the pan.
5. Stirring continuously, increase the heat and bring to the boil.
6. As it starts to boil, add the sweetcorn, stir well and then remove from the heat.
7. If you aren't going to serve it immediately, allow it to cool and then refrigerate.
8. When ready to serve, bring it to the boil one final time, add the water chestnuts and the spring onions and season with salt and pepper.
9. Serve on a bed of noodles or rice.

SERVES 6–8

SLOW-ROASTED LAMB in red wine and onions

Long, slow cooking is definitely the quickest option for a delicious meal. Sounds like a contradiction in terms, but spicing something and leaving it to cook on its own couldn't be easier. You can do everything you need to and when you come home, supper's ready! And your reward for being patient? Tasty lamb!

6 lamb shanks (approximately 2 kg)

½ cup cake flour, seasoned with salt and freshly ground black pepper

little oil for frying

2 large onions, peeled and sliced into thin rings

4 cloves garlic, finely chopped

6 sprigs of fresh rosemary

3 carrots, peeled and sliced into rings

2 cups red wine

1 x 410 g can chopped peeled tomatoes

½ cup water

2 tsp brown sugar

1 Tbsp crushed black peppercorns

2 Tbsp olive oil

salt to taste

1. Wash and dry each shank and sprinkle with the seasoned flour.
2. Heat the oil in a frying pan over a medium heat and fry the shanks until seared to a golden brown colour. Remove from the pan and set aside.
3. Add a little more oil to the pan and fry the onions and garlic until limp.
4. Place the onions, garlic, rosemary and carrots in a roasting pan and arrange the seared shanks in a single layer on top.
5. Preheat the oven to 150 °C.
6. Pour the wine into the pan used for frying the onions and bring to the boil. Scrape all the brown bits off the bottom and simmer until the wine has reduced by about half.
7. Add the tomatoes, water and sugar and again bring to the boil, mashing the tomatoes with a fork as you heat the mixture through.
8. Once boiling, remove from the heat and pour over the meat.
9. Sprinkle with the crushed black peppercorns, drizzle with the olive oil and sprinkle with salt.
10. Cover the roasting pan with foil and bake in the oven for 2 hours.
11. After 2 hours, check on the lamb. If the liquid has cooked out, add 1 cup water, scrape the bottom of the pan and stir well. Baste the lamb with this liquid and continue to cook for another 1½–2 hours, covered.

SERVES 8

power-packed CRANBERRY LAMB

This glossy, tart, scarlet-red berry called the 'cranberry' (sounds like I'm describing a new lipstick on the market) contains the most wonderful healing properties. With all the recipe tasting that goes on in my house, I had forgotten about this recipe until I saw cranberries in a fruit shop and was reminded of it. If it's not the season for cranberries, as it's quite short, dried cranberries work just as well.

200 g fresh cranberries or 100 g dried
3 Tbsp cranberry jelly
1 cup red wine
2 cups chicken stock
3 Tbsp balsamic vinegar
1 Tbsp treacle sugar
2 onions, peeled and sliced into rings
5 sprigs of fresh rosemary
1 shoulder of lamb
coarse black pepper to taste
4 cloves garlic, sliced
35 g fresh mint, chopped
coarse salt to taste

1. Preheat the oven to 180 °C.
2. Place the cranberries, cranberry jelly, wine, stock, vinegar and sugar in a saucepan and simmer until the mixture has reduced by one-third.
3. Place the onions in a roasting pan big enough to fit the lamb comfortably. The roasting pan shouldn't be too big as you don't want all the sauce evaporating too quickly. Don't forget that the lamb will shrink while cooking.
4. Place the sprigs of rosemary on top of the onions and lay the lamb, boney side facing you, on top.
5. Grind coarse black pepper over the lamb and tuck the garlic and mint into all its cracks and crevices.
6. Pour over the reduced sauce and sprinkle with coarse salt.
7. Roast uncovered for about 1 hour. Baste every now and then with the sauce.
8. Reduce the heat to 170 °C, turn the meat, and continue to roast, uncovered, for a further 45–60 minutes until golden brown. Then cover the meat with foil and roast for a further hour.
9. Keep warm on a low heat until ready to serve.
10. Enjoy with roast potatoes, butternut and minted peas or a crisp green salad with fresh cranberries.

SERVES 10–12

ROCH'S 'GARLIC-ENHANCED' rotisserie scotch fillet

It was the first Shabbat where I was to 'meat' my husband's family. My future mother-in-law had made her famous rotisserie Scotch fillet. She knew the exact number of times that meat had to be punctured and filled with garlic to chase away any 'garlic-sensitive' girlfriends! The problem was, this garlic-anaesthetised one was brought up on the bulb and couldn't wait for seconds. New life was breathed into our relationship!

3 kg vacuum-packed Scotch fillet (leave on the bottom shelf of the fridge for 2–3 weeks and ensure that the packaging doesn't blow – it has to fit skin tight)

HERB OIL
1 cup olive or sunflower oil
¼ cup lemon juice
2 Tbsp brown sugar
8 sage leaves
6 sprigs of fresh rosemary
1 bunch of fresh origanum
½ tsp salt
1 tsp coarsely ground black pepper
8 cloves garlic, sliced
1 Tbsp mustard seeds or brown grainy mustard
1 tsp paprika
1 x 60 g pkt onion soup powder

1. Remove the Scotch fillet from its packaging and wash it with cold water. Place the meat in a large Ziploc™ or roasting bag.
2. Place all the ingredients for the herb oil in a bowl and mix well.
3. Gently pour the herb oil over the Scotch fillet and massage the bag so that the meat is entirely coated in the oil.
4. Allow to marinate overnight or for the whole day.
5. Remove the fillet from the bag, place it on a rotisserie bar or skewer and secure it with string. Most ovens and barbecues have rotisseries built in. Make slits in the meat with a sharp-tipped knife and fill with the slices of garlic from the marinade. Go as deep as you want – we sometimes thought there was a piece of fat in the meat and it turned out to be a huge piece of garlic; 'another vlokkie', my husband would say!
6. Cook the fillet for 1½ hours until brown, then allow it to rest for 10–15 minutes. My oven has a timer and switches off automatically after 1½ hours.
7. If you don't have a rotisserie, preheat the oven to 100 °C.
8. Remove the fillet from the bag and ensure it's nicely covered with the herb oil.
9. Either braai, barbecue or fry the meat over a high heat for about 3 minutes per side, until all 4 sides are brown (a total of 12–15 minutes). Remove from the heat and place the meat in a roasting pan. Cover with foil and cook in the preheated oven for 2½–3 hours. Allow to rest for 10–15 minutes.

SERVES 12–14

DALE, MY MACHUTENISTA'S cholent

Although we cannot light a fire on Shabbat, we can derive pleasure from one that was lit before Shabbat. Hence cholent: a stew of meat and potatoes put on to cook before sunset on the eve of Shabbat and eaten at the daytime meal.

We were at my son's in-laws for lunch one Shabbat. 'Now this is a cholent,' my husband exclaimed as he took his first mouthful. 'Well,' said Dale, 'they say a cholent is as good as the visitors who eat it!' Well, TG Rabbi and Rebbetzin Goldman were there too, 'cause we had to be riding on their coat-tails!

1 cup brown rice
1 kg stewing lamb
6 potatoes, peeled and cut into eighths
½ cup dry samp mealies
6 carrots, peeled and sliced into rounds
250 g pumpkin, peeled and cubed
½ cup marinade and basting sauce (Dale uses All Joy)
3–4 Tbsp onion soup powder
enough water to cover

1. Layer the ingredients in a cholent pot (crock-pot) in the order in which they are listed, starting with a layer of rice on the bottom. Cover the lot with a layer of water about 3 cm above the vegetables.
2. Set on a low heat and allow to cook overnight. Don't look at it, squint at it, smile at it or stir it. You must only lift the lid when you are about to serve! Mmm … now that's the spice of Shabbat!

SERVES 8–10

barmi BRISKET

It was my nephew Seth's Bar Mitzvah in Dallas and this delicious brisket was served at the Friday night dinner.

3 kg fresh brisket
2 cups tomato sauce/ketchup
1¾ cups light brown sugar
3 Tbsp prepared yellow mustard
2 Tbsp red wine vinegar

1. Preheat the oven to 180 °C. Place the brisket, fat-side up, in a roasting pan.
2. Combine the tomato sauce, sugar, mustard and vinegar in a bowl, mix well and pour over the brisket.
3. Cover with foil and cook for 3½–4 hours, or until soft. I would check it after 2 hours just to make sure there is enough moisture; if it's getting a little dry on the edges, turn it over and reduce the heat to 170 °C and continue cooking.
4. Remove the brisket and cut the fat off the top. Slice the meat and place back in the sauce in the roasting pan.
5. You can either freeze at this point or keep warm on a low heat until ready to serve.

SERVES 12–14

STUFFED ROLL OF BEEF with a 'bit on the side'

If you don't feel like stuffing your roll of beef, then just order a roll of beef from your butcher, which will come already rolled and tied with string. You can take about 30 minutes off the cooking time if it isn't stuffed.

2–2.5 kg beef flap for rolling (tell your butcher that you want a flat piece of meat to roll yourself)

little olive oil for rubbing and drizzling

8 potatoes, peeled and left whole

2 onions, peeled and quartered

1½ cups water

DRY RUB

1 tsp dried sage

1 tsp dried thyme

1 tsp dried origanum

2 tsp dried rosemary

1 Tbsp mustard seeds or 1 tsp mustard powder

½ tsp garlic powder

1 Tbsp onion soup powder

1 Tbsp brown sugar

1½ tsp paprika

1 tsp crushed black pepper

¼ tsp ground cumin

pinch of chilli powder

½ tsp ground ginger

STUFFING (tip: you can make your own as below or use Ina Paarman's™ stuffing mix, following the instructions on the packet and adding 1 x 410 g can drained mushroom pieces)

½ cup oil or schmaltz

2 medium onions, peeled and finely chopped

500 g mushrooms, sliced

8 fresh sage leaves, finely chopped, or 1 tsp dried

35 g fresh flat-leaf parsley, chopped

2 cups chicken stock, cooled (homemade or available at Nussbaums)

1 x 250 g box cornflake crumbs

salt and pepper to taste

1. Lay the beef out flat on a clean surface and rub both sides with a little oil. Combine the dry rub ingredients and use to coat one side (the outside) of the beef only. Turn the meat over in preparation for stuffing.
2. To make the stuffing, heat the oil or schmaltz in a frying pan and fry the onions until golden brown. Add the mushrooms, sage and parsley and cook until most of the liquid has evaporated. Add the stock and cornflake crumbs and mix well. The stuffing should be quite firm, as it will soften with the juices given off by the meat during cooking. Season with salt and pepper.
3. Preheat the oven to 180 °C.
4. Spoon the stuffing onto the un-spiced side of the beef.
5. Roll up the meat and tie 3–4 pieces of string or roasting bands around it to hold the roll in place. If stuffing oozes out while rolling, just stuff it back in – that's why it's called stuffing!
6. Place the roll in a roasting pan and carefully place the potatoes and onions 'on the side'. Drizzle a little more olive oil over the top of the meat and vegetables.
7. Roast in the oven for 1 hour, uncovered, gently turning the meat halfway through.
8. Remove the pan from the oven, add the water to the pan and cover with foil. Reduce the heat to 160 °C and continue to cook for a further 2 hours. Then reduce the heat to keep it warm. The meat may take a little longer due to the stuffing. The vegetables should be golden brown.

SERVES 8–10

save-my-life BLACK FOREST PIE

Another six for lunch tomorrow! No problem, we'll fill them with Black Forest Pie.

A quick tip: it's always easier to have the ingredients for this pie on standby in your fridge and freezer. It makes life so much easier!

500 g frozen berries
1 cup Shabbat wine
1 x 95 g pkt instant chocolate pudding (I use Osem™)
1 cup non-dairy cream
¾ cup cold water
1 ready-made 22–24 cm-diameter round chocolate sponge cake (available from most kosher bakeries –
    yes, of course you can make your own, if you have the time!)
sugared pecan nuts, and meringues (optional)
sliced strawberries, for decoration
grated pareve chocolate, for decoration

CHOCOLATE GANACHE
75 g chocolate discs (I use Staffords)
3 Tbsp non-dairy cream
1 tsp non-dairy margarine

1. Marinate the berries in the wine overnight, but if you only have an hour, that's better than nothing! Then place them into a strainer and strain well.
2. In a mixing bowl, beat the chocolate pudding, non-dairy cream and water together. Refrigerate until needed. You can buy ready-made chocolate mousse if you'd prefer to do away with the schlep of making chocolate pudding!
3. Cut the cake through the middle, horizontally, into 2 layers.
4. Place one layer at the bottom of a 22–24 cm-diameter springform cake tin.
5. Strain the marinated berries and place half on the first layer of cake.
6. Scoop the chocolate pudding over the berries.
7. Crush the pecan nuts and sprinkle a layer over the top of the chocolate pudding and, if you have any meringues lying around, crush them up and crumble them on top of the nuts.
8. Place the remaining berries on top of the chocolate pudding and cover with the second layer of cake.
9. Make the chocolate ganache by warming all the ingredients in a saucepan over a low heat until the chocolate has melted. Remove from the heat and allow to cool for about 5 minutes before pouring over the cake.
10. Refrigerate immediately for at least 6 hours.
11. When ready to serve, gently remove the cake from the tin and decorate with sliced strawberries around the edges and a pile of grated chocolate in the centre.

refreshing **CRANBERRY PEARS**

Because this was my grandfather's favourite fruit, it became one of my mother's favourite desserts!

    8 pears
    3 cups cranberry juice
    ½ cup sugar dissolved in 1 cup boiling water
    2 cinnamon sticks
    4 cm piece ginger, halved

1. Peel the pears, leaving the stems in, and cut the bottoms off so that they stand flat on the bottom of a deep saucepan. They should fit quite snugly in the pan.
2. Add the cranberry juice, sugar water, cinnamon sticks and ginger.
3. Bring to the boil, then reduce the heat and simmer for 10–12 minutes until the pears are tender, but still firm in their original pear shape. Cooking time depends on the freshness of the pears. Test with a toothpick.
4. Remove the pan from the heat. Place the pears in a glass bowl and cover with the syrup.
5. Allow them to cool at room temperature, turning every so often, so that they are uniform in colour.
6. Refrigerate and serve chilled.

SERVES 8

SHABBAT crème brûlée

A friend of mine, whose stove I don't think is even connected, was coming for Shabbat and asked if she could make anything. Tongue-in-cheek I said, 'Thank you. A crème brûlée would be lovely.' A day or two later, she called to say, 'Shar, this "cream bouquet" that you want, the florist wants to know if they can add some greenery or must it just be plain cream roses?' We did have a good laugh!

8 egg yolks
½ cup castor sugar
2 cups non-dairy cream
seeds of 1 vanilla pod or 1 tsp vanilla extract

SUGAR GLASS
½ cup cold water
1 cup white sugar

1. Preheat the oven to 150 °C.
2. In a large bowl, cream the egg yolks and castor sugar until the mixture is thick and pale yellow.
3. Add the non-dairy cream and vanilla and continue to whisk until well blended.
4. Strain the mixture into a large bowl, skimming off any foam or bubbles.
5. Divide the mixture between 6–8 ramekins.
6. Place the ramekins in a water bath (large pan filled with 3–5 cm of hot water) and bake in the oven for 50–60 minutes until set around the edges, but still slightly loose in the centre.
7. Remove from the oven, but leave the ramekins in the water bath until cool.
8. When cool, remove the ramekins from the water bath and chill for at least 2 hours (or up to 2 days) in the fridge.
9. A traditional crème brûlée is served with a burnt-sugar topping, caramelised with a blowtorch. It usually starts weeping and melting after 45 minutes and is, therefore, a problem on Shabbat. I've overcome it by making sugar glass.
10. Melt the water and sugar in a saucepan on the stove over a low heat. When it starts to turn a lovely caramel colour, watch it closely. As soon as it starts to go a darker brown colour (probably around the edges), don't stir it, but immediately lift it off the heat. Swirl the saucepan by its handle so that the colour distributes evenly, then pour onto a baking tray. It should only take a few minutes to go hard.
11. Break into chards and, just before serving, place the chards on top of the crème custards.
12. My family likes to scoop the crème brûlée up with the chards of sugar glass. But that's only when the queen isn't coming for supper!

SERVES 6–8

JONATHAN'S GRAPEFRUIT sorbet

After a heavy Shabbat meal, a delicious, light, creamy sorbet is all you really want, and need! Here, Jonathan Beare shares with us his famous grapefruit sorbet. If you don't have an ice-cream machine, get one for your next birthday. Believe me, you won't stop making sorbets, because they're just so easy. Then, for the following birthday, you can get a new freezer, just for your sorbets!

6–7 large grapefruit
1 cup sugar
2 egg whites

1. Squeeze the juice from the grapefruits and strain. You will need 1 litre of juice.
2. Dissolve the sugar in the grapefruit juice and refrigerate until cold.
3. Churn in an ice-cream machine* until almost completely set.
4. In a bowl, beat the egg whites until firm.
5. Just before it sets, add the well-beaten egg whites to the sorbet in the machine.
6. Churn for a further 5 minutes and then scoop the sorbet out of the machine with a chilled spoon and into a chilled bowl. (Both spoon and bowl should be placed in the freezer for 10 minutes before the sorbet is ready.)
7. For the best-quality sorbet, one should time it in order to eat the sorbet directly from the machine off a plate that has been in the freezer. If you need to make the sorbet in advance, keep it covered in the freezer, but transfer it to the fridge 10 minutes before serving to ensure that it returns to a smooth, soft consistency.

* If you do not have an ice-cream machine, pour the cold grapefruit juice and sugar mixture into a deep freezer-proof bowl and freeze. After 6–7 hours, remove from the freezer (the centre should still be a little soft for easy blending) and blend the sorbet until smooth, using a hand blender. Alternatively, blend in a food processor. Beat the egg whites until stiff and fold them into the sorbet until well incorporated. Do not use a blender for this! Refreeze. Remove from the freezer 5–10 minutes before serving.

SERVES 10

PESACH

PESACH

On a popularity scale, this festival must fall in the top three! Well, for me anyway!

We start celebrating Pesach with the Seder meal where matzo makes its debut and Baron de Luria, our own homemade vintage, takes centre stage. Year after year we come together at the Seder table where we tell the story of our Exodus from Egypt, and lively songs and beautiful thoughts are shared. Times such as these, in which we connect to our past, keep us united so that we may continue to celebrate from generation to generation.

Seder means 'order' and it's quite ironic that on this night of freedom, we still have to follow an ordered 15-step Seder! But thank G-d it has an order, otherwise we'd still be arguing at the Red Sea: 'You go first!' 'No, after you.' 'Okay I'll go.' 'Why you?'

Pesach is an eight-day festival, but this is where I beg to differ (sorry, but it's in the blood!). For me, Pesach is anything but eight days. It's an intense five weeks of hard labour; scrubbing and cleaning like an obsessive-compulsive maniac! When I start scrubbing those curtains and carpets, believe me, I'm one with my Matriarchs. I must have worked in the launderette of Pharaoh's palace! However, I

must admit that when I sit at that Seder table I breathe a sigh of relief, because mind, body and home have come out of a spiritual cleansing (and physical I might add!) like no other, and I'm ready to face the year with a certain amount of positivity. 'Wiping the slate clean' would seem to be the right idiom.

Some of my warmest childhood memories are those borne out of the strict preparations for Pesach. The 'surgical scrub' and 'changeover' would happen every year. Only once every pot, pan, plate and teaspoon used during the year had been packed away in cupboards and sealed so that not even Houdini's plates could escape, could we bring down the Pesach kitchenware. Up would go the ladders and down from the cupboards would come the crockery and cutlery, unpacked to the beat of a military drum! All this for just eight days of the year and the cooking hadn't even begun! No wonder we called it '*Meshugas* Impossible'. However, the observance of these meticulous laws and customs, which have been observed for thousands of years, is still happening in our own homes today, and hopefully will continue in our children's and grandchildren's homes too.

10 WAYS TO ENJOY 8 DAYS

If Seder *means 'order', then you have to be 'ordernised'.*

1. Just as you prepare your meals for a week's holiday away, so too must you prepare for Pesach. A menu planner works so well.

2. The more you plan and prepare, the more time you'll have on your hands to relax and enjoy Pesach.

3. Make a grocery list – write down how much you use that year, then refer to it when purchasing for the next year. Every year I buy too much and promise to make a list, but don't. While on the subject of lists, make a list of the popular dishes as well.

4. If you need something new, like a potato peeler, buy it immediately. Rest assured, you'll start to make the same thing next year and you won't have one.

5. If you don't have a Pesach kitchen, like most of us, find a spot in your home where you can start preparing food for Pesach. You won't believe what can come out of a patio with a two-plate stove and a trestle table. To think that this came about purely because my children wouldn't allow me to fry fish in the house, so my mother, whose job it is to fry the fish, fried it all outside. I thought: while we're out here with the Pesach utensils, why not make the tzimmes too? Then we made the soup and kneidlach, and so it became 'Pesach from the Patio'!

6. Invest in a blowtorch – it sorts out stovetops, sinks and ovens in no time!

7. Buy catering-size foil and use foil containers. You can always transfer the food into nicer dishes when serving.

8. Clear out your freezer and get your meat early. Don't think: I've ordered so I'll get it. It doesn't always work out that way. I remember a strike at the abattoir one year, two days before Yomtov.

9. Buy 20 kg potatoes and 10 kg onions to see you through the week. For those forever-hungry children, potatoes help!

10. Buy a book like *Countdown to the Seder*. Pesach will be a breeze!

THAI SALMON fishcakes

When you've had your fill of gefilte fish and need a little change, try these.

1 x 418 g can salmon
1 onion, peeled and finely grated
2 Tbsp chopped fresh coriander
1 tsp grated fresh ginger
juice of 1 lime
2 eggs
⅔ cup matzo meal
1 Tbsp desiccated coconut (this takes it to a whole new level)
oil for frying

1. Combine the salmon in its liquid with the rest of the ingredients, except the oil, in a large mixing bowl.
2. Roll into balls and fry in hot oil until golden brown.
3. Serve with sweet and sour sauce (see below).

SWEET AND SOUR SAUCE
⅓ cup lemon juice
⅓ cup golden syrup
1 Tbsp tomato sauce
1 tsp potato flour dissolved in 1 cup cold water
salt and pepper to taste

1. Blend all the ingredients into a smooth sauce and bring to the boil over medium heat or just until it thickens. Check for sweetness – if too sweet add a little more lemon or vice versa.
2. To make it a little fancier, add drained mandarins and crushed pineapple to the sauce. Serve with the fishcakes.

MAKES 12–15

ENGLISH CUCUMBER soup

I always say that, for eight days of the year, one huge pot of soup is enough to keep us going. But somehow, halfway through Pesach, everybody's tired of the same old soup and so I land up making another one. This one normally falls on the other end of the 'traditional' scale.

little olive oil for frying
2 onions, peeled and chopped
2 cloves garlic, chopped
3 potatoes, peeled and chopped
8 cups water
4 cucumbers, washed, deseeded and cubed
2 cups vegetable stock or 2 vegetable stock cubes dissolved in 2 cups boiling water
1 cup non-dairy creamer (I use 1 x 250 ml box Orley Whip™)
2 cucumbers, washed and coarsely grated
2 tsp salt
1 tsp pepper

1. Heat the oil in a soup pot and fry the onions and garlic until soft. Add the potatoes and 4 cups of the water and boil until the potatoes are soft.
2. Add the cucumber cubes and the rest of the water and bring to the boil. Once boiling, reduce the heat, put on the lid and simmer for a further 25 minutes. Remove from the heat.
3. Add the vegetable stock and non-dairy creamer and blend with a hand blender until smooth.
4. Add the grated cucumber, salt (it may need quite a bit as the potatoes absorb a lot of salt) and pepper and return to the heat.
5. Bring to the boil, reduce the heat and simmer for about 10 minutes. Then switch off the heat and allow the soup to stand for a while to develop the flavours.
6. It is meant to be quite a thick soup; however, if you feel it is too thick, add a little more vegetable stock.
7. Sometimes, I finely chop an Israeli cucumber (they're crispier) and sprinkle it cold on top of the soup before serving.

SERVES 10–12

chopped LIVER

While writing this recipe I could almost hear my mother's Kenwood machine droning monotonously as it started its 12-hour Pesach workout. First on the programme was always the chopped liver.

¼ cup oil or schmaltz (okay, so you'll start your diet after Pesach)
4 large onions, peeled and chopped
1 tsp sugar
3 eggs

300 g ready-koshered chicken livers, already grilled
1 chicken stock cube dissolved in ½–¾ cup boiling water
salt and pepper to taste

1. Heat the oil or schmaltz in a large pot and fry the onions and sugar until golden brown. (Caramelising the onions is the secret to that special-tasting liver!)
2. While the onions are frying, hard boil the eggs. Remove the pot from the heat once the onions are brown.
3. Wash the chicken livers in cold water and remove any burnt bits, membranes and sinews. Add the livers to the onions and mix well until all the livers are well coated with onions and oil. Add half to three-quarters of the chicken stock, reserving a bit in case you want to add extra once you have minced everything together.
4. Place the pot back on the stove, bring to the boil, mixing well and scraping all the brown bits off the bottom of the pot. That's where the flavour sits! Once it starts to boil, remove from the heat.
5. Mince the liver and onions with the eggs, using a hand or electric mincer. Add salt and pepper to taste.
6. Should you want a smoother texture, add some of the reserved chicken stock and remince half of the already minced liver. Mix it all together and that should make it smoother.

SERVES 8–10

MY COUSIN JEFF'S kneidlach

How could I not include my cousin Jeff's kneidlach? This is a man so passionate about his family and food (there is a fine line between the two, but only just!) that if he says they're the best, then they're the best! And they're so easy!

4 extra-large eggs
½ cup sparkling water (soda water)
4 Tbsp vegetable oil

1 tsp salt and freshly ground black pepper to taste
1 cup matzo meal

1. In a bowl, whisk the eggs until smooth, then add the sparkling water, oil, salt and pepper and whisk. Add the matzo meal a little at a time and mix until the ingredients are well combined. Cover and refrigerate for 1 hour.
2. Bring a large pot of salted (2 Tbsp salt) water to the boil. Wet your hands and roll the mixture into golf-ball sized balls. Drop them into the boiling water. (I prepare all the balls first, put them on a plate and drop them into the boiling water together. This way all the kneidlach are cooked for an equal amount of time.) Cover and simmer for about 30 minutes. When you see steam starting to escape from the pot, reduce the heat a little so that it's still boiling, but not so vigorously.

MAKES 12–14

My cousin Jeff's kneidlach (left);
Pesach meat blintzes (back right);
Bobba's chremslach (front right)

BOBBA'S chremslach

Every family has their favourite Pesach dish. Ours was Pesachdikke *pancakes. My husband's family favourite was* chremslach. *When I married into the Lurie family, it became my family's favourite too! Make these and your family will love you for life, so will their friends. So make a big batch and get ready to add this to next year's list of things to make. Not that you'll forget ... the family won't let you!*

3 eggs
3 Tbsp oil
3 Tbsp water
matzo meal, enough to make a dough a little firmer than that for kneidlach
   (that sounds a bit like 'a bisl dos and a bisl ...' but you get the picture!)
oil for frying

FILLING
For the filling, use the Pesach Meat Blintzes filling recipe on the opposite page.

1. In a large mixing bowl, combine the eggs, oil and water.
2. Slowly add the matzo meal until a firm dough is formed.
3. Roll the dough into balls a little bigger than golf balls and place on a baking tray sprinkled with matzo meal to prevent them from sticking.
4. Flatten each ball with a rolling pin until it's a little bigger than the palm of your hand, about 6 cm in diameter and 2–3 mm thick.
5. Holding it in the palm of your hand, place a tablespoon of the meat mixture in the centre and close your hand so that the edges meet. Make sure all the edges are sealed so that no meat escapes when it is fried. Shape it any way you like – round or oblong works – just as long as it is sealed with as much meat as you can cram in. Repeat with the remaining balls.
6. Heat the oil in a frying pan and fry the chremslach until golden brown.
7. You can make these in advance and simply reheat on an uncovered baking tray in a 170 °C oven for about 15 minutes, until crisp and warmed through.

MAKES 10–12

PESACH MEAT blintzes

In some communities, it is customary not to eat kneidlach over Pesach. Some observe this for the first two nights, while others refrain for the whole of Pesach. Whatever your minhag may be, these blintzes are the best option with a delicious bowl of homemade chicken soup. My family eat them any time of the day or night, with or without soup. I use this as my blintz recipe all year round as they are gluten free.

4 eggs
1½–2 cups cold water
1 cup potato starch
1 tsp salt
little oil for frying

MEAT FILLING

(If you use soup meat in your soup, then you can either use the cooked soup meat from the soup
 and mince it through with a bit of onion and carrot or you can start afresh as below.)
little oil for frying
1 onion, peeled and grated
2 carrots, peeled and grated
1 kg beef mince
1 tsp potato starch dissolved in ½ cup cold water
salt and pepper to taste

1. In a large mixing bowl, beat the eggs for a minute or two with a fork or hand beater.
2. Add the water, potato starch and salt and continue to beat. You will need to beat the mixture repeatedly, as the potato starch tends to settle on the bottom of the bowl. You may also need to add a little more cold water to prevent the consistency from becoming too thick while the mixture stands.
3. Heat the oil in a frying pan and pour in enough batter to coat the bottom of the pan very thinly. Swirl the mixture around so that it spreads evenly over the bottom.
4. When the batter starts to bubble, turn it over and fry for a further 30 seconds. When cooked, remove from the heat and layer the blintzes, one on top of the other, with a thin layer of foil between each. The first and second blintzes are normally samples. You should get it right by the third, so hang in there. It will be worth it!
5. To make the meat filling, heat the oil in a frying pan and fry the onion until golden brown.
6. Add the carrots and continue to fry until soft, then remove the vegetables from the pan and set aside in a bowl.
7. Add a little more oil to the pan and brown the mince, stirring continuously. When the bottom of the pan has turned brown (caramelisation has taken place), add the potato starch water and continue to stir. To ensure a fuller flavour, be sure to get all the brown bits off the bottom of the pan. Season with salt and pepper.
8. When thoroughly combined, add the onion and carrot and stir well. Use as a filling for the blintzes.
9. Take one blintz at a time, place 2 Tbsp of mince in the middle, pull in the sides so that they meet in the middle and roll up into a cigar shape. Serve immediately.

MAKES 12–14

hands-on PESACH CHUTNEY

This is the sauce that will see you through Pesach. It's an adaptable chutney-ish, monkeygland-ish kind of sauce that you can literally throw over lamb, chicken or beef. My daughter-in-law, Rochi, decided one day to make chutney with the lovely fruit we had picked at my brother's farm. What a girl! Six-week-old twins, no sleep and constantly feeding. All she needed was three pairs of hands! A few hours into the day, the phone rang… 'Sha, this is not for me. Is it ever going to get thick and dark?' Believe me, it does, but when it starts changing colour you really have to be hands on, as it burns very quickly.

little oil for frying
2 cups finely chopped onions
2 heaped tsp crushed fresh garlic (optional)
8 large tomatoes (not too red), chopped
2 mangoes (not too ripe), peeled and chopped
5 cm piece of ginger, grated
1 cinnamon stick
3 green apples, peeled, cored and grated
200 g dried apricots (optional)
1 red chilli, chopped (optional)
2 cups red wine
2 cups sugar
salt and pepper to taste

1. Heat the oil in a large saucepan and fry the onions and garlic until the onions just start to turn brown around the edges. Add the rest of the ingredients.
2. Bring to the boil, then reduce the heat and simmer for 2–3 hours with the lid lying loosely on top. Stir intermittently, especially during the last hour of cooking, but be careful as the sauce could bubble up and spit up at you. Because of the high sugar content, the chutney can catch quite easily towards the end.
3. When it starts to darken, remove from the heat. (It's difficult to give an exact cooking time, as liquids evaporate quicker or slower depending on the size of the pot used, but do it on a day when you're going to be in the kitchen for a few hours.)
4. When cool, place in sterilised 500 ml glass jars with screw-on lids (you'll probably need 3 jars).

MAKES ABOUT 1.5 LITRES

CABBAGE SALAD with white wine vinegar dressing

Salads can be as exciting, colourful and exotic as you allow them to be. I love different textures and that's the reason this salad has the velvety feel of avocados combined with the crispness of a crunchy noodle topping!

1 cabbage, shredded

4 celery sticks, thinly sliced horizontally

2 long red paprika peppers, finely cut lengthways

½ cup roughly chopped fresh flat-leaf parsley or coriander (I prefer coriander)

2 large mangoes, peeled and chopped

3 avocados, peeled and chopped

SALAD DRESSING

1 cup Chilean white wine vinegar

1¼ cups oil

¾ cup sugar

1 tsp salt

1 tsp fresh crushed garlic

freshly ground black pepper to taste

1 vegetable stock cube (I use Telma®)

CRUNCHY NOODLE TOPPING

oil for frying

1 x 250 g pkt Pesach egg noodles (any design except screw shaped)

1. Place the cabbage, celery, paprika peppers and parsley or coriander in a large salad bowl. Toss and store in the fridge.
2. Place the chopped mangoes in a Ziploc™ bag and refrigerate.
3. For the salad dressing, combine all the ingredients in a glass jar or bottle with a tightly fitting lid and shake until the sugar dissolves.
4. Refrigerate until ready to use.
5. For the noodle topping, heat the oil in a frying pan until very hot. Add handfuls of the dry noodles to the hot oil and fry quickly until lightly browned.
6. Remove the noodles and drain on an absorbent paper towel. Allow to cool.
7. Just before serving, place the mangoes on top of the salad and add the avocados.
8. Pour over the dressing, toss gently, then sprinkle the noodles on top.

SERVES 10–12

fennel and cucumber SALAD

I can just hear you saying, 'Mmm ... fennel, now that sounds interesting.' Because that's what I said when I first tried it and what everybody says whenever I serve it! Fennel is crunchy and sweet, with a refreshing taste that blends so well in a salad with minted dressing. While writing this book, I really tried to act responsibly by going 'green'. Most of the pictures were shot outside so that we wouldn't have to use extra electricity. And the excuse for 'stealing' the fennel and mint from my sister-in-law's garden was that I was trying to keep my carbon footprint low by not using my car to go and purchase it! Do you think she bought it?

1 fennel bulb, thinly sliced	DRESSING
8–10 red radishes, thinly sliced	½ cup oil
6 Israeli cucumbers (or any small cucumbers), thinly sliced	¼ cup lemon juice or white wine vinegar
	2 Tbsp chopped fresh mint
3 spring onions, chopped	1 heaped Tbsp sugar
fresh mint leaves to garnish	salt and pepper to taste

1. Combine the fennel, radishes, cucumbers and spring onions in a salad bowl.
2. To make the dressing, whisk the ingredients together in a jug. Pour over the salad, garnish with fresh mint leaves and serve.

SERVES 8–10

fresh HERB SALAD

This wonderful fresh salad is quick and easy to make and is eaten just as quickly and easily! Everybody loves its freshness.

1 English cucumber, peeled and diced	2 spring onions, chopped
2 firm tomatoes, diced	¼ cup chopped fresh parsley
1 green pepper, deseeded and diced	salt and freshly ground black pepper to taste
1 celery stick, thinly sliced	4 Tbsp olive oil
¼ cup chopped fresh coriander	juice of 2 lemons (about ¼ cup)
1 red onion, peeled and chopped	1 Tbsp sugar

1. Toss the cucumber, tomatoes, green pepper, celery, coriander, red onion, spring onions and parsley in a salad bowl and season with salt and pepper.
2. In a separate bowl, mix the oil, lemon juice and sugar. Pour over the salad and toss to coat. Refrigerate, covered, and serve cold.

SERVES 8

Fennel and cucumber salad

Mexican matzo salad

MEXICAN MATZO salad

This is great for those forever-hungry teenagers over Pesach!

GARLIC MATZO STRIPS	2 Tbsp lemon juice
½ cup oil	1 tsp crushed fresh garlic
1 tsp crushed fresh garlic (if garlic isn't your thing, use some dried herbs instead)	salt and pepper to taste
pinch of salt	FRESH SALSA
4 matzo sheets	1 large red onion, peeled and chopped
	2 medium tomatoes, chopped
	1 bunch of fresh coriander, finely chopped
GUACAMOLE	1 English cucumber, finely chopped
2 avocados, peeled and chopped	salt and pepper to taste

1. Preheat the oven to 180 °C. To make the garlic matzo strips, mix the oil, garlic and salt in a bowl and allow to stand for a few minutes. Paint each sheet of matzo with the garlic oil and place on a baking tray. Bake for 5–10 minutes until golden and crispy. Meanwhile, make the guacamole and salsa.
2. For the guacamole, blend or mash together all the ingredients and refrigerate until needed.
3. For the salsa, mix all the ingredients in a bowl and drain off any excess juices by pressing the mixture into a colander or sieve.
4. Break the baked matzo sheets in half and layer with the guacamole and salsa as shown, or simply arrange on a platter with bowls of guacamole and salsa, for people to use the matzo as scoops.

SERVES 6–8

PESACH crunchies

If your family is anything like mine then a salad has to be divine! It has to be crisp, veggies must blend and not offend and the dressing must be light and tart, but made with a sweet heart. These croutons are wonderful on top of any salad.

1 cup potato flour, sifted	1 tsp bicarbonate of soda
1 cup cold water	1 tsp salt
½ cup cake meal	oil for frying

1. Combine the potato flour and water in a bowl and mix well until smooth. Add the cake meal, bicarbonate of soda and salt and mix until combined. Place the mixture in a squeezy bottle.
2. Heat the oil in a frying pan over a medium to high heat. Squeeze slightly larger than peanut-sized amounts of the mixture into the frying pan and fry until golden brown.
3. If you find that you are battling to squeeze out the mixture, add a little more water and shake the bottle well, or simply make the hole in the bottle a little bigger.

MAKES LOTS

GNOCCHI

Roast potatoes are a thing of the past! Serve with ready-made pasta sauce or as an accompaniment to steak.

4 large potatoes	1 heaped tsp baking powder (I use Gefen)
3 eggs	1 heaped tsp salt
3 Tbsp potato flour	oil for frying

1. Boil or microwave the potatoes (whole and in their skins) until soft. Allow to cool, then peel and coarsely grate into a large bowl. You can also use a potato ricer.
2. Whisk the eggs and add them to the potatoes with the potato flour, baking powder and salt. Mix well to form a soft, but not too sticky, dough. Sprinkle some potato flour onto a board and start rolling pieces of the dough into long thin sausages – about 1 cm in diameter. Slice these into 2 cm pieces.
3. Heat the oil in a frying pan and deep-fry the gnocchi until golden brown.
4. They can be served immediately or reheated (uncovered) in the oven to regain their crispness.
5. Instead of frying, you can cook the gnocchi in a pot of boiling salted water. Put only five or six into the pot at a time, as you want the water to boil continuously. When they are cooked, they will float to the top.

SERVES 10–12

CHOL HAMOED steaks

It was the morning of the first night of Pesach and my son had told his friends that we were burning chometz at 9 a.m. The neighbourhood arrived and so did the fire engines. My son had lit such a huge fire that the trees uprooted and ran, the birds flew north, the neighbours put up a 'For Sale' sign and we cooked meat on the fire the entire day! So this one's for you, Boruch, our Pesach Pyromaniac! This is so good that we eat it all year round, and I really mean that!

2 pepinos or 1 pawpaw, peeled and deseeded	4 cm piece ginger, grated
2 Tbsp red wine vinegar	6 steaks
1 Tbsp sugar	little oil for drizzling
	freshly ground black pepper and salt to taste

1. In a food processor, blend the pepinos or pawpaw with the red wine vinegar, sugar and ginger until smooth.
2. Place the steaks in a large Ziploc™ bag and cover with the pepino/pawpaw mixture. Mush it around so that the steaks are evenly coated and leave to marinate. Do not let them marinate for more than 3 hours, otherwise they go like chopped liver. After 2½–3 hours, remove the steaks from the bag, discard the pepino/pawpaw mixture and rinse the steaks very well under cold running water. Pat dry.
3. Place the steaks in a single layer, side by side, in a rectangular roasting dish and drizzle with oil. Sprinkle with some coarsely ground black pepper. Turn the steaks over and again drizzle with oil and sprinkle with black pepper.
4. Braai or fry the steaks to perfection. Just before removing from the heat, brush with a little more oil, remove from the heat and allow to stand for 10 minutes, loosely covered in foil. Sprinkle with a little salt and plate immediately.

SERVES 6 (MAYBE 4, BECAUSE SOMEBODY WILL WANT SECONDS!)

Chol HaMoed steak with gnocchi

SCOTCH FILLET with rosemary baby potatoes and horseradish cream

The most important thing to remember here is that when you receive your Scotch fillet, leave it in the fridge for at least 12 days before you freeze or use it. Don't worry, I leave mine for at least two to three weeks and, boy, am I alive and kicking! This recipe ensures that you get your meat early! I have to side with the butchers at this time of the year. There's method to my madness in this recipe and that is not to leave your Pesach meat delivery to the last minute.

2 kg vacuum-packed Scotch fillet
½ cup oil
2 Tbsp crushed black peppercorns
1 kg baby potatoes
few sprigs of fresh rosemary
oil for roasting potatoes

HORSERADISH CREAM
1 tsp sugar
1 tsp potato flour
½ cup cold water
½ cup non-dairy creamer
pinch of salt
1 Tbsp fresh horseradish, grated or 1½ Tbsp Nussbaums bottled horseradish, drained

1. Preheat the oven to 200 °C.
2. Place the meat on a roasting rack in a roasting pan, cover in the oil and rub all over with the crushed peppercorns so that it's evenly covered.
3. Roast the meat in the oven, uncovered, for 1¼ hours (for every extra kilogram of meat, increase the cooking time by 30–40 minutes). If you don't have a roasting rack in your roasting pan, turn the roast over halfway through cooking.
4. Meanwhile, prepare the rosemary baby potatoes. Place the potatoes (skin on or off) in a roasting bag with the rosemary and a few glugs of oil. Place on the side of the roasting pan with the meat when there is 1 hour of cooking time remaining.
5. When done, remove the meat from the oven, cover in foil and leave to stand for 15 minutes while you make the horseradish cream. The horseradish cream can be made the day before and warmed up when needed.
6. Combine the sugar, potato flour, water, non-dairy creamer and salt in a mixing bowl and whisk well.
7. Pour the mixture into a saucepan and heat through, whisking all the while, until it starts to thicken. Remove from the heat, add the horseradish and stir.
8. Serve with the meat and rosemary baby potatoes.

SERVES 8–10

PESACH lasagne

Just when you thought it was safe to relax, suddenly you have a couple of hungry mouths to feed. Remember, everybody's home for lunch on Pesach. There's nowhere to hide over these eight days! This is the perfect Pesach backup for those in-between meals.

little oil for frying

2 onions, peeled and chopped

1 green pepper, deseeded and chopped (optional)

1 tsp sugar

1 kg beef mince

2 cups Nussbaums chicken soup (this can be substituted with 2 chicken stock cubes dissolved in 2 cups water, but there's nothing like the real thing!)

1 x 115 g can tomato paste

2 ripe tomatoes, peeled, deseeded and chopped (drop them in boiling water for 30 seconds to loosen the skins)

1 tsp crushed garlic

handful of fresh basil (about 35 g), chopped

salt and pepper to taste

6–8 matzo sheets

WHITE SAUCE

2 heaped Tbsp potato flour

2 cups non-dairy creamer (I use 2 x 250 ml box Orley Whip™)

2 cups cold chicken soup or stock

1. Heat the oil in a large frying pan and fry the onions and green pepper (if using) until soft. Add the sugar and stir.
2. Add the mince and fry until cooked through.
3. Add the chicken soup or stock, tomato paste, tomatoes, garlic, basil, salt and pepper and stir, bringing it to the boil.
4. Once bubbling, reduce the heat and simmer for about 10 minutes with the lid lying loosely on top. You want the sauce to be quite moist as the matzo will absorb some of the moisture while cooking.
5. Meanwhile, make the white sauce by dissolving the potato flour in the non-dairy creamer and cold chicken soup or stock. Bring to the boil in a saucepan over a medium to high heat, whisking all the while. When it starts to thicken, reduce the heat, whisk for a further minute, and then remove from the heat. The sauce should have a smooth, pourable consistency. If it's too thick, add a little more soup or stock.
6. Preheat the oven to 180 °C.
7. To assemble the lasagne, place a layer of white sauce in a foil container or ovenproof dish, followed by a layer of mince, then a layer of matzo. Continue to layer in that order, ending with the white sauce. Bake in the oven for 25–30 minutes until bubbling and golden brown on top. If you want, you can freeze this dish before baking. When ready to use, simply defrost and bake as per the recipe.

SERVES 6

MOCK SCHNITZELS with mushroom and red wine sauce

These are wonderful as they can be dressed up or down! Serve them with a beautiful mushroom and red wine sauce and fresh vegetables, or fry them and store in the fridge for the 'perpetually starving over Pesach' family to nosh on!

½ cup cake meal

1 cup matzo meal

2 Tbsp chicken stock powder

1 tsp salt

½ tsp pepper

12 beef minute steaks or chicken schnitzels

3 eggs, beaten

oil for frying

MUSHROOM AND RED WINE SAUCE

400–500 g mushrooms, sliced

½ cup red wine

2 Tbsp mushroom stock powder

2 x 125 ml sachets Orley Whip™ Cook 'n Crème

2 tsp potato starch dissolved in 1 cup cold water

1. Place the cake meal, matzo meal, chicken stock powder, salt and pepper in a bowl and mix until well combined.
2. Dip each steak into the beaten eggs and then into the crumb mixture.
3. Heat the oil in a frying pan and fry the steaks until golden brown. Drain well on absorbent paper towels.
4. To make the sauce, fry the mushrooms in a frying pan until soft.
5. Add the red wine and continue to cook for 3–4 minutes.
6. In a bowl, combine the mushroom stock powder, Orley Whip™ and potato starch water. Mix well and add to the mushrooms and wine.
7. Bring to the boil, then reduce the heat and simmer for a minute or two.
8. Serve the steaks on mashed potato, smothered in the mushroom and red wine sauce.

SERVES 5–6

PESACH pot roast

Isn't it funny how you associate certain pots in your cupboard with certain meals? There's one in particular that I only associate with pot roasts. I know it's one of my mother's pots that she probably inherited from my granny, because it looks like a 'that generation' kind of pot. It's so heavy that when you pull it out you have to have a damn good reason for doing so. And so, to give it its due, I make a real old-fashioned, hearty pot roast in it.

2 kg raisin-rib roast (chuck roast off the bone)
little potato flour for dusting
little oil for frying
3 onions, peeled and sliced into rings
250 g mushrooms, sliced
1 beef stock cube (I use Telma® or Osem™)
water, as much as necessary
4 carrots, peeled and sliced into 0.5 cm-thick rounds
4 large potatoes, peeled and quartered
1 tsp salt
½ tsp pepper

1. Pat the roast dry with a paper towel and rub with a light dusting of potato flour.
2. Heat the oil in a deep pot and brown the roast on all sides. Allow the meat to get as brown as possible, as a dark rich colour enhances the end result.
3. Remove the roast from the pot and set aside in a dish deep enough to hold the juices that it will give off.
4. Meanwhile, to the same pot, add a touch more oil and fry the onions for a few minutes until soft. As you stir the onions, try to scrape all the little bits of caramelised beef off the bottom of the pot.
5. Add the mushrooms and beef stock cube and continue to fry for a few more minutes. Return the roast (with its juices) to the pot and add enough water to go about a third of the way up the sides.
6. Bring to the boil and continue to scrape all the bits off the bottom of the pot. Once boiling, add the carrots and reduce the heat. Cover and allow the pot roast to simmer for about 1¾ hours. Just check once or twice during the cooking process to ensure that all the water hasn't evaporated.
7. Add the potatoes and a further 2 cups of water. The water doesn't have to cover the potatoes; there needs to be just enough water in the pot to keep an ongoing flow of moisture in the pot. Season well with salt and pepper and bring to the boil. Then reduce the heat, give it a gentle stir (so as not to break up the potatoes) and simmer for a further 1½ hours. The end result should be a succulent roast, with moist vegetables that have absorbed all the natural and delicious flavours in which they have been simmering.
8. Serve with butternut or gem squash. My husband loves it with horseradish.

SERVES 8–10

risk-it **BRISKET**

After all the cleaning, comes the cooking! But it's almost a relief, because at this stage it's all behind us. We know that our kitchens are finally Pesachdik and everything is kosher. Once the ovens and sinks have been blowtorched, out comes my brisket.

Don't look at this recipe and go: 'Oy vey, more than three ingredients, I'm not going to risk it!' Make it – you won't regret it!

2–2.5 kg fresh brisket
2 Tbsp potato starch
little oil for frying
1 cup chopped onions
1 tsp crushed fresh garlic
2 tsp finely grated fresh ginger
250 g fresh mushrooms, sliced
½ cup red wine
1 beef stock cube dissolved in ½ cup hot water
1 cup Coca-Cola®
1 tsp coffee dissolved in ½ cup hot water
2 Tbsp onion soup powder (I use Osem™ or Telma®)
1 Tbsp tomato paste (I use Gefen)

1. Preheat the oven to 180 °C.
2. Rub the brisket with the potato starch. Heat a little oil in a large pot or frying pan (just enough to cover the bottom) and fry the brisket on both sides until nicely browned. Be careful not to burn the bottom of the pot, as you need to add stock a little later.
3. Once browned, remove the brisket and set aside to cool.
4. Add a little more oil to the pot and fry the onions until lightly browned. Add the garlic and ginger and fry for another minute or two.
5. Add the mushrooms and simmer, stirring occasionally, until most of the liquid has evaporated. Then add the wine and beef stock and bring to the boil. Boil for a minute or two, stirring continuously.
6. Add the Coca-Cola®, coffee, onion soup powder and tomato paste. Stir well and, when it starts to boil, remove the pot from the heat.
7. Place the brisket in a roasting pan and pour over the mushroom gravy. Cover and cook in the oven for 2½–3 hours, until soft. A bigger piece needs longer to cook.
8. The gravy should be almost like a glaze. If it is too watery, cook for a little while longer, uncovered, to allow more of the liquid to evaporate.

SERVES 10

forget-me-not BRISKET

I always forget to serve at least one thing on Pesach or Shabbat, so I had to call this dish 'Forget-me-not Brisket', because it's so good that you really don't want to do that! However, it can easily be forgotten, because once in the oven you don't have to think about it for seven hours!

3 kg pickled brisket
400 g apricot jam
3 Tbsp red or white wine vinegar
1 x 115 g can tomato paste
1 cup water
1 Tbsp grated fresh ginger or ½ tsp ground
1 heaped tsp horseradish (bottled)
1 Tbsp crushed peppercorns
3 bay leaves

1. Preheat the oven to 150 °C.
2. Place the washed brisket in a roasting bag.
3. Combine the remaining ingredients in a bowl. Mix well and pour into the bag with the brisket. Tie firmly, place in a roasting pan and bake for 6–7 hours.
4. After 6 hours, check to see if the meat is cooked by inserting a long-length carving fork through the centre of the brisket. If it goes through smoothly without any problem, it's ready.
5. Serve with pumpkin and roast potatoes.

SERVES 12–14

beef BOURGUIGNON

No matter how early I place my order, I always land up with the offcuts over Pesach. Remember ... the shoemaker goes without shoes ... and so this recipe was born. (Now I place my order under a pseudonym! But then again, I also send myself flowers on Valentine's Day!)

2 kg beef, cubed (about 3 x 3 cm)
1 x 750 ml bottle (3 cups) semi-sweet red wine
little oil for frying
500 g baby onions, peeled
2 cups peeled and sliced carrots (about 5 mm-thick rounds)
1 cup chopped celery
3 cloves garlic, crushed
1 Tbsp chopped fresh thyme or 1 tsp dried
½ cup roughly chopped fresh parsley
250 g button mushrooms
salt and pepper to taste
little potato flour for coating
2 Tbsp tomato purée (I use Gefen)
2 beef stock cubes dissolved in 2 cups boiling water

1. Marinate the meat in 2 cups of the red wine, covered and in the fridge, for about 8 hours or overnight.
2. Remove the meat from the wine, strain off any excess and discard the wine.
3. Heat the oil in a large frying pan and fry the onions until lightly browned.
4. Add the carrots, celery, garlic, thyme and parsley and continue to cook for 10–15 minutes, stirring every now and then.
5. Add the whole mushrooms and continue to cook until the liquid starts to evaporate.
6. Season with salt and pepper and mix well. Remove the vegetables from the pan and set aside.
7. Dab the meat dry with a paper towel, place on a board or tray and sprinkle with a little potato flour. Mix well to coat.
8. Return the pan to the heat, add a little more oil and fry the meat in small batches until golden brown all over.
9. Preheat the oven to 160 °C.
10. Once all the meat is browned, return the vegetables and meat to the pan.
11. Add the remaining red wine, tomato purée and beef stock and bring to the boil for about 5 minutes, then reduce the heat and simmer for a further 15 minutes.
12. Pour the mixture into an ovenproof dish, cover with a lid and cook for 1¾–2 hours. If, after this time, you feel that there is too much liquid, remove the lid, raise the oven temperature to 180 °C and continue to cook for a further 30 minutes, allowing the liquid to reduce.
13. Serve on a bed of mashed potato or potato gnocchi (see page 68).

SERVES 8–10

BEEF and drunk prunes

I also like to call this 'Fusion Tzimmes'. Why? Because this is a fusion of my mother's and my mother-in-law's tzimmes recipes! Maybe I should have called it 'Confusion Tzimmes'! Oy, let's not blow anybody's fuse and just cook! When I start making this recipe, I know I'm finally in the Pesach-production mode.

250 g pitted prunes	2 Tbsp sugar
1 cup Kiddush wine	2 litres Nussbaums chicken stock
2 cinnamon sticks	500 g carrots, peeled and sliced into
little oil for frying	1 cm-thick rounds
2 kg top-rib roast or 2 top-rib flaps	500 g pumpkin, peeled and cubed
2 onions, peeled and	500 g potatoes, peeled and cubed
finely chopped	salt and pepper to taste
1 Tbsp finely grated fresh ginger	1 heaped Tbsp potato flour dissolved in
2 Tbsp golden syrup	1 cup cold water

1. Allow the prunes to marinate in the wine and cinnamon overnight.
2. Heat the oil in a large pot big enough to hold the meat. Brown the outside of the top-rib roast. Remove from the pan and set aside.
3. To the same pot, add the onions and ginger and stir until the onions start to darken.
4. Add the syrup and sugar and stir until dissolved.
5. Add the marinated prunes along with the wine and cinnamon sticks.
6. Bring to the boil, then reduce the heat and simmer for about 10 minutes.
7. Add the chicken stock and return the meat to the pot. Add the carrots, pumpkin and potatoes and season with salt and pepper.
8. Simmer for a further 1½–2 hours. Check regularly to ensure that there is still liquid.
9. After 2 hours, add the potato flour mixture and stir quickly to prevent lumps from forming.
10. Bring to the boil and cook until the mixture thickens.
11. Preheat the oven to 170 °C.
12. Remove the meat, slice it and divide it between two large ovenproof foil containers or dishes, then cover with the sauce and vegetables. I make this dish in advance and at this point refrigerate or freeze it until ready to serve. When required, defrost and bake uncovered until the sauce starts to bubble and the top starts turning golden brown. Reduce the heat, cover again and keep warm.

SERVES 12

STUFFED BREAST OF LAMB with honey-glazed vegetables

I have a standing joke with my doctor's wife, Jane Klein. Every year at Pesach, she phones me to say, 'There'll be 12 extra at your Pesach Seder this year.' We laugh and she asks if there's anything new to make, but I know how the conversation is going to end. Just as it always does: 'Ach, you know what, Sharon? I'm just going to make your beef and stuffed breast of lamb again. I make it every year and they all love it, so they'll just have to love it again! Okay, thanks. Bye.' So Jane, this one's for you, until we speak again.

3 lamb breasts (ask your butcher
to cut a pocket for the stuffing)
marinated in the juice of 3 lemons
for a few hours or overnight

STUFFING

2 cups chopped onions
little oil for frying
250 g mushrooms, sliced
10–12 sage leaves
2 Tbsp finely chopped fresh parsley
1 cup Nussbaums chicken stock or
1 chicken stock cube dissolved in
1 cup boiling water
1 cup matzo meal
salt and pepper to taste

SPICE RUB
1 tsp paprika

2 tsp crushed black pepper
1 tsp salt
needles of 3–4 sprigs of fresh rosemary
3 cloves garlic, crushed, or 1 tsp garlic salt
1 tsp ground cumin
1 tsp ground ginger or 1 Tbsp grated fresh

HONEY-GLAZED VEGETABLES

4–6 cups fresh vegetables: baby potatoes,
baby onions, cubed red, green and
yellow peppers, sliced aubergines,
sliced marrows and any other of your
favourite vegetables
¼ cup honey
¼ cup olive oil
3 Tbsp red wine or balsamic vinegar
1–2 Tbsp chopped fresh thyme
salt and pepper to taste

1. While the breasts are marinating, prepare the stuffing. Fry the onions in oil until golden brown. Add the mushrooms, sage and parsley and continue frying until the liquid from the mushrooms starts to evaporate.
2. Add the chicken stock and stir well. Bring to the boil and remove from the heat.
3. Add the matzo meal, salt and pepper and stir well. Allow to cool. The stuffing can be refrigerated overnight.
4. Prepare the spice rub by combining all of the ingredients in a small bowl.
5. When ready to roast, preheat the oven to 180 °C. Drain the breasts of any excess lemon juice, rub all over with the spice rub and fill with the stuffing. Place in an ovenproof dish, cover and roast for 1 hour.
6. While the meat is cooking, prepare the vegetables. Place the vegetables in a roasting bag. Mix the honey, olive oil, wine or balsamic vinegar, thyme, salt and pepper and pour over the vegetables.
7. After an hour, uncover the meat, add the vegetables (in the sealed roasting bag) and continue to roast both meat and vegetables for a further 45–55 minutes, until golden brown.
8. After 45 minutes turn the meat over carefully (you don't want the stuffing falling out) and continue to cook, meat and vegetables uncovered, for another 35–40 minutes.

SERVES 10–12

THAI GREEN CHICKEN curry

A friend of mine who doesn't eat processed products, only fresh, during Pesach, asked me to come up with a green recipe that she could make plenty of before Pesach and freeze. So, here's how I tried to oblige.

1.5 kg chicken schnitzels
little potato flour for dusting
6 Tbsp oil
2 onions, peeled and finely chopped
2 red peppers, deseeded and sliced
2 cups vegetable or chicken stock
milk of 1 coconut (½–¾ cup)
(On the top of the coconut are three holes. Pierce these with a sharp knife, turn the coconut upside down over a glass and allow the milk to flow out. Alternatively, grate as much of the coconut as you can, pour boiling water over it and let it steep for about 1 hour. Then strain it into a bowl. You can also use 1 cup desiccated coconut covered in 1 cup boiling water then strained.)

THAI GREEN-CURRY PASTE
2 chillies, sliced in half and deseeded
2 lemon grass stems, chopped
35 g fresh coriander
2 cloves garlic, peeled and finely chopped (optional)
6 cm piece root ginger, peeled and finely chopped
4 spring onions, chopped
juice of 1 lime
1 tsp finely grated lime rind
1 tsp ground cumin (optional)
about 25 curry leaves

1. Cut the chicken schnitzels into 1 cm strips and roll lightly in potato flour. Set aside.
2. Prepare the Thai green-curry paste by blending all the ingredients in a food processor.
3. Heat half of the oil in a large saucepan and sauté the onions and red peppers for 2 minutes.
4. Stir in the Thai green-curry paste and cook for 1 minute.
5. Add the stock and coconut milk and bring to the boil. Reduce the heat and simmer for 10 minutes, then remove from the heat.
6. In a separate frying pan, heat the rest of the oil and sauté the chicken strips for 4–5 minutes until they are nicely browned. Remove from the heat and add to the saucepan of Thai green-curry sauce. Leave to stand for about 30 minutes to absorb the flavours. Reheat when ready to serve.
7. Serve on a bed of mashed potato.

SERVES 6–8

Nanna's Pesachdikke pancakes

NANNA'S *PESACHDIKKE* pancakes

Certain aromas and smells can really jolt the memory. I was frying pancakes last Pesach and my son walked into the kitchen and said, 'This smells like Nanna's house in Durban.' We used to lock up the house and go down to Durban every Pesach. We'd arrive Erev Pesach, once everything had been done, and leave eight days later! What a pleasure! The smell of cinnamon and sugar melting on hot pancakes would wake us up almost every morning.

3 eggs
1 cup cold water
1 cup matzo meal
oil for frying
1 cup sugar mixed with 1 Tbsp ground cinnamon

1. Combine the eggs, water and matzo meal until well blended. The consistency should be a pourable one.
2. Fry in oil until golden brown on both sides, remove and drench with cinnamon sugar. Some people also like to pour a little golden syrup on first, then drench with cinnamon sugar.
3. Serve immediately with fresh berries.

MAKES ABOUT 8 (SIDE-PLATE SIZE)

RHONA'S ginger cake

It must have been the happiest day of Rhona Karpelowsky's life when I told her that it was the last time I would be asking her for her Pesach ginger cake recipe. Every year I swear that I will put it away safely, but then I can't remember where!

1 tea bag	2 tsp bicarbonate of soda
1 cup boiling water	1¾ cup cake meal
6 eggs	1 cup potato starch
1 cup sugar	3 tsp ground ginger
1 cup oil	1 tsp ground cinnamon
1 cup golden syrup	

1. Place the tea bag into the boiling water and allow to steep for at least 10 minutes.
2. Meanwhile, cream the eggs and sugar until light in colour.
3. Beating continuously, add the oil, followed by the syrup.
4. Add the bicarbonate of soda to the tea, then add this to the egg mixture and continue to beat.
5. Add the cake meal, potato starch, ginger and cinnamon and mix well.
6. Pour the batter into a greased loaf tin and bake for 1 hour. When done, switch off the oven and leave the cake in for a further 10 minutes.
7. As another option, turn it into a sticky toffee pudding by heating ⅓ cup golden syrup, ⅓ cup water and 1 Tbsp pareve margarine. Once they have melted together, give it a good whisk and drizzle over the ginger cake as it comes out of the oven.
8. This also makes a wonderful chocolate cake. Simply replace the ginger and cinnamon with 2 Tbsp cocoa powder.

toffee apple PESACH CAKE

We had just finished shooting the photograph of this cake when our food stylist turned to me and said, 'This cake looks so delicious, I have to try it.' Her facial expressions and groans of sheer delight as she ate the first slice and began cutting the next left my brother and I both speechless! Not because of her outward signs of satisfaction or the fact that she wanted to take the whole cake home, but because who enjoys or even wants to eat a Pesachdikke cake when it isn't even Pesach?

5 large Granny Smith apples
1 cup water
100 g pecan nuts, coarsely chopped
1 cup sugar (brown is better if available for Pesach)
1 Tbsp ground cinnamon
4 eggs
1 cup sugar
½ cup oil
1 tsp vanilla essence

1 cup cake meal
½ tsp bicarbonate of soda dissolved in
¼ cup water
½ cup raisins

TOFFEE SAUCE
½ cup cold water
¾ cup sugar
125 ml non-dairy creamer

1. Preheat the oven to 170 °C.
2. Peel, core and cut the apples into eighths.
3. Place the apples in a small to medium-sized saucepan, cover with the water and bring to the boil.
4. Once boiling, switch off the heat, stir and cover with a lid. Allow the apples to stand and soften in the hot liquid until cool.
5. Mix the pecan nuts, sugar and cinnamon in a bowl until well combined and set aside.
6. In a separate bowl, beat the eggs and sugar until light and creamy.
7. Add the oil and vanilla essence and continue to beat until well combined.
8. Stir in the cake meal and bicarbonate of soda and blend well.
9. Pour half the batter into a greased 20–24 cm-diameter cake tin and sprinkle over half of the pecan mixture.
10. Combine the apples and raisins and spoon half over the pecan layer.
11. Pour over the other half of the batter, followed by the remaining apples and raisins. Sprinkle over the remaining pecan mixture and bake in the oven for 1 hour, then switch the oven off and leave it in for another 15–20 minutes.
12. While the cake is baking, make the toffee sauce. Bring the water and sugar to the boil. Once it starts to turn caramel in colour, remove from the heat, add the creamer and mix well.
13. Remove the cake from the oven and pour over the toffee sauce. Serve at room temperature.
14. This cakes keeps well in the fridge, covered in cling film or tightly fitted foil.

GELATO DI CIOCCOLATA with nutty chocolate sauce

This delicious chocolate ice cream is so close to the real thing that an Italian friend of ours, Adriano Benjamino, asked me how I managed to get his mother's secret recipe! And it's Pesachdik *too!*

10 eggs, separated	**NUTTY CHOCOLATE SAUCE**
1½ cups sugar	**100 g pareve dark chocolate, broken into pieces**
400 g pareve dark chocolate	**½ cup boiling water**
¼ cup oil	**1 heaped tsp peanut butter**
	1 Tbsp golden syrup
	1 x 125 ml sachet Orley Whip™ Non-dairy Cream

1. To make the ice cream, beat the egg yolks and 1 cup of the sugar until light and creamy. Use an electric beater, because this can take a while! Meanwhile, melt the chocolate in a double boiler (or place a medium-sized saucepan into a slightly larger one half-filled with boiling water).
2. When melted, slowly add to the egg-yolk mixture and then add the oil. Continue to beat until very well combined.
3. Separately beat the egg whites until firm, while gradually adding the remaining sugar.
4. Fold the eggs whites into the chocolate mixture and mix well so that there are no little bits of egg white still visible.
5. Pour into a suitable container, such as a freezer-proof glass bowl or foil container, and freeze for at least 48 hours.
6. To make the nutty chocolate sauce, melt the chocolate, boiling water, peanut butter and syrup in a double boiler or in the microwave. When completely melted, remove from the heat and whisk in the Orley Whip™.
7. Serve warm or cold over the chocolate ice cream.

SERVES 12–15

PESACH almond snaps

These are so yummy you'll want to make them all year round.

½ cup Cardin margarine	**pinch of salt**
½ cup sugar	**Orley Whip™ Non-dairy Cream and fresh**
100 g ground almonds	**berries to serve**
1 Tbsp potato flour	

1. Preheat the oven to 170 °C.
2. Melt the margarine and sugar in a saucepan over a medium heat. Once the sugar has dissolved, add the almonds, potato flour and salt and mix well. Remove from the heat and allow to cool (about 20 minutes).
3. Line a baking tray with baking paper and drop teaspoons of the cooled mixture onto the paper about 12 cm apart.
4. Bake for 8–10 minutes until lightly browned.
5. Allow the biscuits to cool on the baking tray for about 5 minutes before transferring to a cooling rack.
6. Sandwich together with Orley Whip™ and fresh berries, or use as wafers with ice cream.

MAKES ABOUT 25

light SYRUP LACYS

These are sweet, crispy and light-as-a-feather in-betweeners.

    batter (see page 67)
    oil for frying
    lots of golden syrup

1. Make the batter as for the Pesach Crunchies (see page 67), but increase the water to 2 cups. The batter will now be smoother and runny enough to squirt out of a plastic squeezy bottle.
2. Pour enough oil into a frying pan so that it comes halfway up the sides of the pan. Heat the oil and, once hot, gently squirt some of the batter into the pan in any design you desire – circles, squiggles, spirals, whatever! Fry until golden brown. It's easier to do one at a time as they cook very quickly.
3. When cooked, remove from the oil and drain on an absorbent paper towel before arranging on a plate or in a bowl.
4. Warm the golden syrup so that it is easier to pour and drench your shapes for a sweet, crispy treat.
5. You can actually use this batter to fry chicken and fish – just don't drench them in syrup!

MAKES A PYRAMID PLATEFUL

MATZ ADO about something

This delicious pudding can even be served for tea.

5 large matzo sheets	CUSTARD CRÈME
125 g non-dairy margarine	**6 egg yolks (keep the whites for meringues!)**
1 cup sugar mixed with 1 Tbsp	**2 cups non-dairy creamer**
ground cinnamon	**1½ cups water**
2 large Granny Smith apples,	
peeled, cored and finely grated	TOPPING
1 cup raisins	**100 g pecan nuts, roughly crushed**
	3 Tbsp sugar

1. Spread each sheet of matzo with margarine.
2. Place a sheet of matzo in a lightly greased ovenproof dish (square foil containers work well).
3. Sprinkle with a little cinnamon sugar, followed by a little grated apple and a handful of raisins.
4. For the custard crème, beat the egg yolks, non-dairy creamer and water until well combined. Pour 1 cup of the liquid over the apple and raisin layer.
5. Top with another sheet of matzo and repeat the layers until you've used up all of the matzo sheets.
6. Top with the pecan nuts and sugar.
7. Refrigerate the pudding for at least 12 hours to allow the matzo to soften and absorb the flavours.
8. Bake in the oven at 180 °C for 25–30 minutes.

SERVES 6–8

Light syrup lacys

bon voyage **BROWNIES**

When I returned from a recent trip to London, my cousin, naturally worried about the state of airline food, gave me a batch of brownies 'just in case'. What made them even better was that they were gluten free and perfect for Pesach!

125 g Cardin margarine	4 eggs, separated
¾ cup sugar	½ tsp bicarbonate of soda
¼ cup cocoa powder, sifted	1 x 125 ml sachet Orley Whip™
¼ cup potato starch, sifted	Non-dairy Cream
100 g almonds, ground	150 g pareve chocolate

1. Melt the margarine and sugar in a saucepan over a low heat.
2. When the sugar has dissolved, remove from the heat and add the cocoa powder, potato starch and ground almonds. Mix well and then set aside to cool for about 20 minutes.
3. While the chocolate mixture is cooling, beat the egg whites until stiff.
4. Preheat the oven to 170 °C.
5. Slowly add the egg yolks and bicarbonate of soda to the cooled chocolate mixture and mix well.
6. Fold in the egg whites.
7. Pour the mixture into a large square cake tin or two 24 x 16 cm foil containers and bake in the oven for 50 minutes for a single large cake or 35 minutes if divided into two smaller cakes, or until a toothpick inserted into the middle comes out clean.
8. Remove from the oven and allow to cool in the tin.
9. Place the Orley Whip™ and 100 g of the chocolate into a saucepan and melt over a low heat, stirring continuously.
10. Pour the warm sauce over the entire cake, allow to cool and cut into squares.
11. Grate the remaining chocolate and sprinkle on top of the brownies.

MAKES 12

guava sorbet and **WARM FRUIT SALAD**

I love making fancy puddings for the Sedorim. It's a challenge to create something different every year! But we also have to be realistic – does anybody really have space for dessert after the Seder? My family all seem to think so, so for them I will continue to challenge myself! Oy, the guilt! However, for those less demanding who feel like something light, this works well.

GUAVA SORBET
4 cups water
1 cup sugar
24 guavas, cut in half

1. Heat the water and sugar in a saucepan until the sugar dissolves.
2. Add the guavas and bring to the boil. When the guavas have softened, remove the pan from the heat and blend until smooth, either in a food processor or a blender.
3. Using a piece of muslin cloth or a very fine sieve, strain the guava purée and discard the pulp and pips.
4. Pour the strained guava purée into a freezer-friendly container and freeze for about 5 hours.
5. After 5 hours, blend the sorbet again until smooth. The sorbet shouldn't be frozen through yet and should still be soft enough for you to immerse a hand-blender into it. Or, spoon the sorbet back into a food processor or blender and blend until smooth. Refreeze.
6. Serve with the warm fruit salad (see below).

WARM FRUIT SALAD
2 x 310 g cans mandarin orange segments in syrup
2 x 567 g cans pitted litchis in syrup
1 x 410 g can peach slices in syrup
1 x 425 g can sliced mangoes in syrup
any berries in season
any canned fruit that has the Pesach hechsher (kosher certification)
1 heaped tsp potato starch
½ cup red wine

1. Drain all the fruit, conserving the juices.
2. Place the fruit in one bowl and the juices (equivalent to 2 cups of liquid) in another.
3. Add the potato starch and red wine to the juices and mix well.
4. Pour the juice mixture into a saucepan and bring to the boil over a medium heat. It should thicken a little.
5. Add the fruit to the hot juice mixture, give it a gentle stir and then turn off the heat.
6. Serve with the guava sorbet.

SERVES 12–14

SHAVUOT

SHAVUOT

As a child, I always received a new pair of shoes for Pesach and I guarded that shoe box with my life, because that was the box I would decorate for the annual 'fruit box' competition on Shavuot, seven weeks later! (*Shavuot* means 'weeks' – we had to wait seven weeks, hence the name, to receive the Torah at Mount Sinai after our departure from Egypt, Passover.) The festival of Shavuot is also known as Yom Ha Bikkurim, the festival of fruits. I loved decorating my children's fruit boxes too, but I had to stop being an over-enthusiastic mother when the rabbi announced that 'Mrs Lurie has taken first prize for her son Darren's fruit box'. There was my little Darren, aged 3, sobbing his heart out thinking his chocolate was going to his mommy! The following year they put their own fruit and veggies into a box that they had decorated. It looked like they were moving home, but all three boys carried it into shul together. Oy, did I cry! That box was the most beautiful and special box ever made! One of my life's many lessons.

Traditionally, we should eat dairy products on Shavuot, one of the reasons being that upon receiving the Torah we immediately became obligated to its laws of kashrut. Since we did not have time to prepare kosher meat, we ate dairy instead. However, Shavuot is a Yomtov and on a Yomtov we never substitute a meat meal with milk, as we want to fulfil the commandment 'And you shall rejoice'. For most people, there is no 'rejoicing' without meat! Our rabbi always laughs and makes it quite clear when he announces this fact that he is not being paid by the three butchers in our community to do so!

Cheesecake for breakfast is good and blintzes at the shul brocha are fine, but, for a Yomtov meal, you can't beat meat. In fact, I normally serve a dairy soup in the playroom, followed by a meat meal in the dining room. Fair is fair!

coconut KABELJOU

When I was a child we had a boat. No, not a boat you would find in the south of France. Ours was more like a miniature fishing trawler! Every Sunday the whole family was on The Romany *fishing. My father would sit with four fishing rods in front of him while the rest of us relaxed and chatted, not even noticing that we had a bite. Until one day I was nearly pulled overboard my rod bent over so far. 'I've definitely got a body with legs in cement here,' I screamed. Of course my father took over, because I could never land this one and there it was, a beautiful shimmering kabeljou that to this day I have never seen as big in any fishery.*

Being the loyalist (loyal to meat that is) that I am, I have to add that this dish is also wonderful if you want to substitute chicken fillets for kabeljou. I would first fry or grill my chicken on both sides to give it that golden-brown glow.

1 bunch (4–6) spring onions, chopped
1 red pepper, deseeded and chopped
1 green pepper, deseeded and chopped
1 stick lemon grass
1 bunch fresh coriander, finely chopped
2 cloves garlic, crushed
20–25 small curry leaves
1 small red chilli, chopped, or 1 tsp hot chilli sauce (see page 25)
little oil for frying
1 cup canned coconut milk
1 tsp ground turmeric
1 tsp yellow mustard seeds
1.5 kg kabeljou, skinned, filleted and cut into 8 pieces (if you can't get kabeljou,
   use your favourite white fish)

1. In a large frying pan, fry the spring onions, peppers, lemon grass, coriander, garlic, curry leaves and chilli in a little oil until soft.
2. Add the coconut milk, turmeric and mustard seeds and bring to the boil. Reduce the heat and simmer for 4–5 minutes.
3. Wash the fish and dry well with paper towels.
4. You have two options here. Either you can place the fish in the pan with the sauce and allow it to cook through or you can place the fish under the grill first to brown it a little. You only need to brown the top of the fish, not both sides. Place the browned fish in the pan, ensuring that the brown side faces you, then cover with the sauce.
5. Once the fish is in the pan, don't turn it, but rather spoon the sauce over it while it cooks through.
6. Serve on a bed of Basmati rice.

SERVES 8

salmon À LA HELEN

My publishers had to twist my arm to add fish to this book. But admittedly, my cousin Helen didn't have to twist it too hard when she insisted I taste this dish. Just the smell that permeated the room when she unwrapped the foil got me going!

2–2.5 kg side of salmon
1 cup soy sauce
1 bunch fresh coriander, roughly chopped
1 knob freshly grated ginger (a little larger than your thumb)
⅓ cup honey
2 chillies, chopped

1. Preheat the oven to 220 °C.
2. Place a large piece of foil on a baking tray and place the fish, skin-side down, onto the tray. Draw the sides of the foil up and around the fish, but don't close just yet.
3. Combine the remaining ingredients in a jug and pour over the fish.
4. Scrunch the sides of the foil together in the middle and bake for 20 minutes. Remove from the oven and allow to stand, sealed, for about 10 minutes before opening. Open the foil carefully so as not to burn yourself on the steam.
5. Serve hot or cold. I like to serve it as a starter with a light cabbage salad.

SERVES 8

'rushin' EASY-PEASY SOUP

It was a normal day: I was rushing around, thinking about supper, but taking it no further than that. What a surprise to get home and find that my daughter (who, like me, is a 'soupie groupie') had made a wonderful pea soup! Needless to say, it got its name not only from the Russian sausage sprinkled on top, but from the kind of day I was having too!

2 large onions, peeled and roughly chopped

2 celery sticks, chopped

2–3 cloves garlic, crushed

little oil for sautéing

1 heaped tsp hot curry powder

12 large mint leaves

1 kg frozen peas

6 cups homemade chicken stock*

1 x 250 ml box Orley Whip™ Cook 'n Crème

salt and pepper to taste

4 Russian sausages, diced

1. In a soup pot, sauté the onions, celery and garlic in a little oil.
2. Keep stirring and, after 2–3 minutes, add the curry powder and mint leaves.
3. Add the peas and chicken stock and bring to the boil.
4. Once boiling, reduce the heat and simmer for about 1 hour.
5. Remove from the heat, add the Orley Whip™ and blend with a hand blender or in a food processor until smooth.
6. Add salt and pepper to taste.
7. Just before serving, fry the diced sausage until golden brown and sprinkle on top of each bowl of soup.

SERVES 8

* I always (okay, nearly always!) use homemade stock. At least once a month, I make a huge pot of chicken stock. I then fill 1-litre Ziploc™ bags with it and freeze them until needed. You wouldn't believe how quickly they go! Sneeze and you get a bowl of chicken soup! However, if you've been rushin' with no time to 'stock up' then either buy ready-made chicken soup from Nussbaums or use 4 chicken stock cubes dissolved in 6 cups of water for this recipe.

good old-fashioned cream of **MUSHROOM SOUP**

Shavuot is during winter in South Africa. A hearty soup, therefore, does it for most. This soup is made with a non-dairy creamer, but for those who would like to start their meal off with a milk soup, just substitute it with butter, cream and milk.

2 Tbsp non-dairy margarine
2 onions, peeled and finely chopped
½ tsp crushed garlic
750 g mushrooms, sliced
freshly ground black pepper to taste
3 Tbsp cake flour
2 cups soy milk
2 cups non-dairy creamer (I use Orley Whip™ Cook 'n Crème)
2 cups cold water
salt to taste

1. Heat the margarine in a large saucepan and fry the onions until limp.
2. Add the garlic and mushrooms and continue to fry until most of the moisture has evaporated. While frying, grind over some black pepper.
3. Remove from the heat, sprinkle the flour over the mushrooms and stir well.
4. Add the soy milk, non-dairy creamer and water and whisk until well combined.
5. Return to the heat and bring to the boil, whisking all the while.
6. Once it starts to boil and thicken, reduce the heat and simmer for 2–3 minutes, stirring continuously.
7. Using a hand blender, blend the soup for about 5 seconds. Alternatively, transfer it to a food processor and pulse a few times just to bring it all together. It is meant to be quite a thick soup.
8. If you removed it from the pan to blend, return it and bring to the boil again. Switch off the heat, add salt to taste and allow the soup to stand for about 1 hour to absorb all the flavours.

SERVES 8

JIM'S RED WINE-'LESS' chicken

While writing this book, I contacted family who I hadn't seen in many years. I wanted to know more about my Granny Gracie who passed away very young. My mother only knew her mother-in-law for two very short years, but the memories she had were so warm and wonderful.

I had pictured a kind, warm, gregarious, generous lady who entertained and cooked beautifully. Then I received an email from my cousin who proceeded to tell me that the first five attributes were accurate, but the last one, her cooking, she left for her cook Jim to take care of. She taught him everything. Ah, okay. I felt better; she was a good delegator! This chicken recipe was her favourite, but she couldn't understand why it wasn't as good as it was originally, until she discovered that Jim was drinking the wine instead of using it in the dish!

little oil for frying
1 whole fresh chicken, cut into portions
1 onion, peeled and chopped
1 carrot, peeled and sliced
250 g mushrooms, sliced
½ tsp crushed fresh garlic
few sprigs fresh thyme
2 Tbsp finely chopped parsley
2 cups dry red wine
salt and pepper to taste
½ cup chicken stock (if necessary)

1. Preheat the oven to 170 °C.
2. Heat the oil in a frying pan and fry the chicken portions until brown on all sides.
3. Remove the chicken from the pan and place in a roasting dish.
4. To the same pan, add the onion and carrot and fry until soft.
5. Add the mushrooms, garlic, thyme and parsley and continue to cook for a few minutes.
6. Add the red wine and bring to the boil. Turn down the heat and simmer until reduced by a quarter.
7. Pour the sauce over the chicken, season with salt and pepper, cover with a lid and bake for 45 minutes.
8. Remove the lid and bake for a further 40–60 minutes. If it looks like the chicken is drying out, add ½ cup chicken stock and give it a gentle stir to loosen all the brown bits from the bottom of the dish.
9. The end result should be a lovely, dark-brown, glazed chicken.

SERVES 6

instant tan **STICKY CHICKEN**

Use any part of the chicken you enjoy for this recipe. We love the wings and drumsticks. There are two stages to this recipe, but they're so simple it's really worth doubling up on the effort!

18 chicken wings or 12 drumsticks
½ cup fresh lemon juice
1 tsp crushed fresh garlic
1 tsp finely grated fresh ginger
1 tsp salt
freshly ground black pepper to taste

SAUCE
¾ cup Nussbaums BBQ marinade (or any supermarket brand)
¾ cup chutney
½ cup tomato sauce
1 Tbsp Nando's Hot Peri-Peri Sauce (optional, for a bit more spice)
30 g pareve chocolate (I use Staffords 70% Cocoa Discs)
(Chocolate? Yes, chocolate. The chocolate helps to speed up the chicken's tan, while the rest of the ingredients in the sauce help to keep it well moisturised. Think about it: If you put chocolate in your meat, you won't have to make dessert!)

Stage 1

1. Place the chicken pieces in a large Ziploc™ bag.
2. Combine the lemon juice, garlic, ginger, salt and pepper. Add this to the chicken and *shochel* (shake) the bag, ensuring all the pieces get coated.
3. Place the bag in the fridge and allow the chicken to marinate overnight or for an entire day.

Stage 2

1. Preheat the oven to 200 °C.
2. Make the sauce by combining all the ingredients in a small saucepan over a medium heat and stirring until the chocolate has dissolved. Alternatively, microwave on full power for 2 minutes.
3. When ready to cook, remove the chicken pieces from the bag, pour off the juices and pat them dry. Place the chicken pieces in a bowl and pour over the sauce.
4. Mix well so that the chicken pieces are evenly coated and lay them next to one another in a roasting pan.
5. Roast for 35–45 minutes, turning over the chicken pieces halfway.
6. Reduce the heat to 170 °C and continue to bake for a further 30–40 minutes.
7. Keep turning them every so often, to ensure they are evenly bronzed. You don't want them to look like a bad instant-tan job, all white in the creases!
8. If they're taking too long to brown, put them under the grill for a few minutes, but keep basting.

SERVES 6

ISAAC'S SHERRIYUMMY beef

Isaac was my grandfather's right-hand man who started off as his cook and later became his driver. My grandfather was a doctor and, unlike Jim (see page 101), Isaac had to be stone-cold sober 24/7. So there was never a problem with the taste of Isaac's beef dish! The sherry was always spot on – hence us calling it 'sherriyummy' beef and not 'sherriyukkie' beef!

1.5 kg beef, cut stroganoff-style
chopped parsley and cashew nuts to serve

MARINADE
½ cup oil
½ cup soy sauce
¼ cup sherry or Shabbat wine
½ cup tomato juice
2 Tbsp brown sugar
1 onion, peeled and grated
1 tsp crushed garlic
1 Tbsp grated ginger
1 Tbsp cornflour

1. Place the beef in a marinating dish. Combine all the marinade ingredients in a bowl, mix well and pour over the meat. Allow to marinate for a minimum of 3 hours.
2. Heat a skillet and fry the meat in small batches – too big a batch causes the meat to boil instead of brown.
3. If there is any marinade left in the marinating bowl, stir ½ cup of water into the marinade and pour it into the pan in which you were frying the meat. Bring to the boil and allow to simmer for about 5 minutes. Pour over the meat.
4. Serve on a bed of rice and sprinkle with chopped parsley and cashew nuts. (Microwave the cashew nuts first to crisp them up, but watch them as they can burn easily.)

SERVES 6

mushroom and spinach **PASTA BAKE**

Isn't it funny how, in our mind's eye, when we think pasta we think 'milk' or lovely macaroni cheese or Fettuccine Alfredo, always a rich, creamy dairy dish. Well, a non-dairy pasta dish can still be creamy, velvety and smooth, with just as much flavour and moisture, and with the added bonus of being able to be served as a side dish to meat.

250 g (½ pkt) pasta (tagliatelle or linguine)

2 Tbsp pareve margarine

2 large onions, peeled and chopped

400 g mushrooms, sliced

400 g baby spinach leaves, well washed

2 Tbsp cake flour

2 cups soy milk

1 cup non-dairy creamer (I use Orley Whip™ Cook 'n Crème)

1 tsp salt

freshly ground black pepper to taste

1 mushroom or vegetable stock cube dissolved in 1 cup boiling water

1. Cook the pasta according to the packet instructions.
2. Preheat the oven to 180 °C.
3. Meanwhile, heat the margarine in a frying pan and fry the onions until golden brown.
4. Add the mushrooms and spinach and cook until most of the moisture has evaporated.
5. Remove from the heat and allow to cool a little.
6. Dissolve the flour in the soy milk and non-dairy creamer and mix well.
7. Add the flour, soy milk and non-dairy creamer mixture to the mushrooms and spinach and mix well.
8. Return to the heat and bring to the boil, whisking all the while.
9. As soon as it starts to bubble, add the salt, pepper and stock and continue to whisk. Once it starts to boil again, remove from the heat and set aside.
10. Drain the cooked pasta and place in a well-greased roasting dish.
11. Pour the mushroom and spinach sauce over the pasta, mix gently and bake, uncovered, until golden brown.
12. Once it starts to turn brown, remove the dish from the oven, cover in foil and keep it warm – there should be enough moisture to prevent it from drying out if it's kept in a warm place.

SERVES 8–10

PEAR, CRANBERRY AND crystallised-ginger cobbler

Why do people hesitate the minute they see a recipe containing ginger? Nobody will even know it's ginger; they'll just think it's delicious! If they ask, just tell them you 'peared-up' cranberries – it's the truth!

1 large can pear halves, roughly chopped (retain the juice)
½ cup dried cranberries
½ cup sugar
⅓ cup fresh orange juice
2 Tbsp coarsely chopped crystallised ginger
1 Tbsp custard powder

2 Tbsp cornflour
½ tsp finely grated orange peel (optional)
1 cup cake flour
½ Tbsp baking powder
¼ tsp salt
3 Tbsp chilled non-dairy margarine
¾ cup non-dairy creamer
2 Tbsp brown sugar

1. Preheat the oven to 190 °C.
2. Mix the pears, pear juice, cranberries, sugar, orange juice, ginger, custard powder, cornflour and orange peel (if using) in a large bowl. Transfer to a baking dish.
3. In a separate bowl, combine the cake flour, baking powder and salt.
4. Add the margarine and, with the tips of your fingers, make a fine crumble.
5. Add the non-dairy creamer and mix lightly until a moist dough forms.
6. Break off bits of the dough and drop them over the fruit, covering as much as you can. If you battle to get the dough off your fingers, just dip your fingertips in water. That should help.
7. When all the dough is used up, sprinkle the brown sugar over the top and bake for 40 minutes.
8. Serve warm with pareve vanilla ice cream.

easy LOKSHEN PUDDING

Give me pasta any day of the week. Give me raisins every day of the week. Give me a lokshen pudding and you're my friend for life!

500 g dry tagliatelle pasta	1 cup soy milk
¾ cup sugar	1 cup water
6 Tbsp non-dairy margarine	1 cup raisins
4 whole eggs plus 2 extra yolks	4 Tbsp brown sugar mixed with 1 Tbsp
1 cup non-dairy creamer	cinnamon to sprinkle on top

1. Cook the pasta according to the packet instructions.
2. Drain and place in a large greased ovenproof dish.
3. Preheat the oven to 180 °C.
4. Melt the sugar and margarine in a saucepan until the sugar dissolves, then remove from the heat and allow to cool.
5. Meanwhile, whisk the eggs, extra yolks, non-dairy creamer, soy milk and water until well combined. Add to the cooled sugar and margarine and mix well.
6. Sprinkle the raisins over the cooked pasta, followed by the egg and sugar mixture.
7. Finally, sprinkle the brown sugar and cinnamon on top.
8. Bake for 40–45 minutes. Remember that when you take it out of the oven, the pasta will still absorb some of the liquid, so don't overcook it as it can dry out.

SERVES 8–10

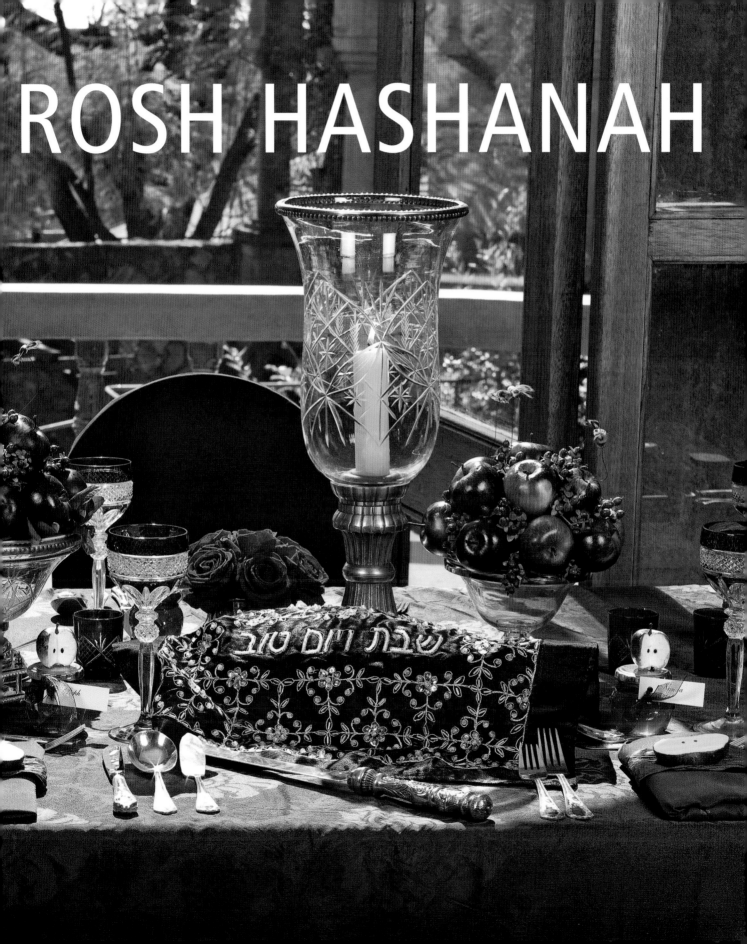

ROSH HASHANAH

ROSH HASHANAH

Rosh Hashanah literally means 'head of the year' and is referred to as the Jewish New Year. From the start of Rosh Hashanah, through the Ten Days of Repentance, we are taken into one of the holiest days of the year, Yom Kippur. These are days of serious introspection. Even as I write this, a certain kind of mood seems to envelope me; one of respect, awe and, dare I say it, fear!

For me, the sounding of the *shofar* (the ram's horn) is the key ingredient in my Rosh Hashanah recipe for the soul. There is something about the cry of the *shofar* that sparks off an internal emotion that no written word can ever explain. The blows of the *shofar* serve not only to awaken us from our spiritual slumber, to get back on track and start afresh, but also represent, among other things, the trumpet blasts at the coronation of a king. On Rosh Hashanah, we proclaim G-d as our one and true King.

Just as our souls need nourishing, so do our bodies so that we have the strength to perform all our New Year's resolutions. There are so many beautiful and traditional foods to do this over the High Holy Days.

The first thing that comes to mind are apples dipped in honey. Both symbolise our desire for a sweet year.

We also eat carrots (in tzimmes), because carrots in Yiddish are *meren*, which means 'increase', and we want all good things to increase in the New Year!

We also have a 'new fruit' on our table; something tasted for the first time since it was last in season. I always try to get a pomegranate, because, just as a pomegranate is packed with beautiful seeds, so too we hope to have a year packed with as many *mitzvoth* and good deeds.

A lot of people have the head of a fish on their Yomtov table (sometimes a whole cooked fish or just a head filled with gefilte fish), symbolising the 'head' of the year.

Challahs (kitkes) at this time of the year normally contain raisins (for sweetness) and are round to symbolise the cycle of life. I like to plait mine in the shape of a crown to symbolise our proclamation of G-d as our King. Just before baking, I sprinkle my challahs with cinnamon sugar and then, just before eating, we dip them in honey. Talk about an overkill on the sweet stuff!

the great outdoors, **FISH BALLS**

Everybody has their favourite fish balls. Some like them sweet, some savoury, but most like them the way their mother did them.

My children won't allow me to fry fish in the house, as they say the odour lingers for a little too long. So my mother comes over and fries it outside, on a two-plate stove. She puts on a plastic shower cap and prays that nobody comes to visit! We do it twice a year, Rosh Hashanah and Pesach – the rest of the year we buy fish already fried.

A tip I learnt from a friend in Atlanta: buy frozen gefilte fish loaves (available at Tiberius Fish Emporium), cut them into 1 cm-thick slices and fry the slices until golden brown. Serve with a sweet chilli and mayonnaise sauce. Quick tip: you can also paint them with a little sweet chilli sauce and bake them according to the instructions on the packet.

2 kg hake, skin removed
4 large onions, peeled and quartered
4 large carrots, peeled and cut into chunks
handful of fresh parsley
2 cups cornflake crumbs or 1½ cups matzo meal
1 Tbsp salt (fish loves and needs salt – remember where it came from?)
pinch of white pepper
4 eggs, lightly beaten
1 cup water (fish also loves water)
oil for frying

1. Mince the hake, onions, carrots and parsley through an electric mincer attachment.
2. Mix well and add the cornflake crumbs, salt, pepper, eggs and water.
3. The mixture should be quite soft; if it's too firm the fish balls become hard.
4. With wet hands, take heaped tablespoons of the mixture and roll into balls, a little bigger than golf balls.
5. Place them onto a baking tray lightly dusted with matzo meal or cornflake crumbs.
6. Place enough oil in a frying pan so that it comes halfway up the sides. Heat the oil and carefully fry the fish balls until golden brown.
7. When cooked, remove with a slotted spoon and drain on paper towels.
8. Serve cold with horseradish. (I know horseradish is tart and we shouldn't eat it on Rosh Hashanah, but I double-up on the honey with the challah to balance it out! I love my chrain!)

MAKES ABOUT 40

SALMON-CUPPED AVOCADO and cucumber mousse

When there is a large crowd and a lot of food to get through, it's sometimes easier to plate a starter individually. The hero on the plate is the salmon cup, but some asparagus and artichokes drizzled in a light vinaigrette enhance the look.

1 cucumber, peeled and finely grated
2 avocados, peeled and chopped
½ cup mayonnaise
1 tsp lemon juice
salt and pepper to taste
2 tsp gelatine (I use Hanamal Pure Gelatin Kosher Fish Gelatin Powder)
200 g smoked salmon leaves
1 English cucumber to decorate

1. Place the grated cucumber in a sieve over a bowl and squeeze out any excess juice. Keep the juice for later. It should be about ½ cup; if not, add water to make up the difference.
2. In a separate bowl, mash the avocados, mayonnaise and lemon juice and season with salt and pepper.
3. Warm the cucumber juice in the microwave for 10 seconds, then stir in the gelatine.
4. Add this to the avocado and mayonnaise mixture and quickly mix together.
5. Add the grated cucumber, stir well and spoon the mixture into paper cookie cups set in a muffin pan. Refrigerate until set.
6. When ready to use, place each cup upside down on a plate, peel off the paper (it doesn't matter if there are crinkles on the mousse) and drape with the smoked salmon leaves.
7. Using a potato peeler, slice the skin off the English cucumber and then slice another piece the length of the cucumber. Wrap this around the salmon cup, securing it with a toothpick or twig of rosemary. Repeat with all of the salmon cups. If you use a toothpick, place a baby tomato on the end just to make it look a little more elegant!
8. Decorate the plates with asparagus, lemon wedges and sliced avocado, and grind over some black pepper.

SERVES 6–8

TRIPLE A SALAD (avocado, asparagus and apple salad)

I'd been putting off clearing out a cupboard in my house for quite some time. We had the cupboard doors replaced so I was forced finally to do it. What a wonderful trip down memory lane! Under old photographs, in-between books, wrapped in a tablecloth, I found a collection of recipes. Paging through it I found this recipe, which I immediately remembered and in fact regretted that I hadn't made in twenty-odd years. After all these years, I wouldn't want to regret not sharing it with you.

½ cup honey

½ cup apple cider vinegar

1 small purple onion, peeled and sliced

½ tsp dry mustard powder

½ tsp salt

1 cup vegetable oil

2 large apples (I use Pink Lady)

250 g fresh asparagus, cut into 1 cm slices

1 x 400 g baby spinach (any other spinach is too bitter)

2 avocados, peeled and sliced

½ cup dried cranberries

1. Combine the honey, vinegar, onion, mustard, salt and oil in a glass bowl.
2. Blend with a hand blender or in a food processor for about 2 minutes until well combined.
3. Check for sweetness – you may prefer to add a little more honey.
4. Chop up the apples (skin on) and immediately place them into the honey dressing to prevent them from going brown.
5. Place the cut asparagus in a separate bowl and cover with boiling water. Count to 10 and then discard the boiling water and immediately fill the bowl with ice-cold water. Wait 10 seconds and discard that too.
6. Place the spinach on a platter, followed by a layer of asparagus, half the apples in honey dressing, all the avocado and the other half of the apples. Finally, top with the cranberries.

SERVES 8–10 (MORE IF IT'S A SIDE SALAD)

SHANA TOVA vegetable soup

I usually serve my perogen with chicken soup (page 23), but my husband prefers a light vegetable soup with his perogen! So this is his Yomtov soup. 'Not too much,' he always says, 'just enough for the perogen to get their toes wet!'

oil for frying	8 baby marrows, cut into 2 cm slices
2 onions, peeled and chopped	2 litres water
5 celery sticks, very thinly chopped	3 Tbsp vegetable stock powder
3 leeks, sliced	1 tsp salt and pinch of pepper
6 carrots, peeled and chopped	handful of fresh parsley
500 g butternut, peeled and cubed	

1. Heat the oil in a large pot and fry the onions, celery and leeks until soft. Add the carrots, butternut, baby marrows and water and bring to the boil. Reduce the heat and simmer for 2 hours.
2. Add the vegetable stock powder, season with the salt and pepper, add the parsley and transfer to a food processor or use an immersion or hand blender. Blend the soup until smooth – it shouldn't be too thick.
3. Reheat before serving.

hasslefree HASSLEBACK BEEF

This piece of meat is the perfect cut for the job it's about to perform. Many cuts in all different shapes and sizes were interviewed for the position as Hasslefree Hassleback Beef. But it was round bolo, with its compact, smooth and wonderful texture that kept getting called back to the boardroom table, where it was finally hired.

1 vacuum-packed round bolo	1 bunch flat-leaf parsley, finely chopped
½ cup oil	1 Tbsp crushed black pepper
2 tsp crushed fresh garlic	2 Tbsp soy sauce

1. Leave the vacuum-packed meat in the fridge for 10 days.
2. Remove the meat from the packaging and slice it three-quarters of the way through in 1 cm-thick slices.
3. Combine the rest of the ingredients in a bowl.
4. Pour a tablespoon of the mixture between each slice of meat and the rest over the top.
5. Wrap in foil and allow to marinate overnight.
6. When ready to cook, remove from the foil and try to keep the herbs and garlic packed around the meat.
7. Fry or braai over a high heat on all sides until golden brown and cooked according to preference.
8. Allow it to stand and 'relax' for about 10 minutes, covered in foil, then serve.
9. Serve with baked potatoes and your favourite salad or vegetables.

SERVES 3–4

Hasslefree hassleback beef

'now this is outstanding' BRISKET

The best part of this dish is that it's not even brisket – it's pickled hump! And even better, it's leaner than brisket!

2–2.5 kg pickled hump
2 litres ginger ale
3 bay leaves
1 cup treacle sugar

1 x 350 g bottle preserved ginger syrup
  with pieces
2 Tbsp grainy mustard

1. Wash the hump in cold water to get rid of the excess pickling salt.
2. Place the ginger ale in a deep pot and add the meat and bay leaves.
3. Bring to the boil, then reduce the heat and simmer for 2 hours with the lid on.
4. Meanwhile, prepare a roasting pan by placing a large sheet of foil running vertically over the roasting pan and another running horizontally.
5. Preheat the oven to 180 °C. Make the glaze by combining the treacle sugar, preserved ginger syrup (with pieces) and mustard in a small saucepan. Heat through until the sugar dissolves.
6. Remove the meat from the ginger ale and place in the centre of the foil-lined roasting pan.
7. Pour the glaze over the meat, pull the foil up on all sides to balloon over the meat and scrunch all the loose ends together to seal the meat in the foil.
8. Roast for 1 hour, then open the foil carefully so as not to burn yourself.
9. Baste the meat well and continue to roast, uncovered, for a further 45 minutes, basting every now and then.
10. Once most of the moisture has cooked out and the meat has a beautiful golden-brown sticky glaze, remove from the oven. This can be served with potato kugel (see page 30) and red ribbon cabbage (see below).

SERVES 8

red ribbon CABBAGE

1 red onion, peeled and chopped
little oil for frying
½ cup quartered pitted prunes
1 kg red cabbage, finely shredded
2 Tbsp redcurrant jelly
2 Tbsp red wine vinegar

1 chicken or vegetable stock cube
  dissolved in ½ cup water
1 Tbsp cornflour dissolved in juice of
  1 orange
salt and ground black pepper to taste

1. Fry the onion in a little oil until soft. Add the prunes, continue to fry for a minute, then add the cabbage and continue to cook for a minute or two, stirring all the time.
2. In a jug, combine the jelly, vinegar and stock and pour over the onion and cabbage. Stir well and simmer for 10–15 minutes. Add the cornflour dissolved in orange juice and bring to the boil, stirring until thickened.
3. Season with salt and pepper, remove from the heat and reheat when ready to serve.

SERVES 8

slow cooker **PULLED BEEF**

Slow-cooking is the new convenience cooking – that's for sure. Haven't you had days when your brisket cuts like a dream into perfect slices and the next time you make it, it shreds? Well, here's the next best thing since sliced brisket!

oil for frying

2 kg fresh brisket

4 onions, peeled and sliced into rings

1 cup cold water

6 potatoes, peeled and halved (optional)

1 cup Nussbaums BBQ marinade (or any supermarket brand)

1 cup tomato sauce

2 Tbsp apple cider vinegar

⅔ cup brown sugar

⅓ cup golden syrup

2 Tbsp Dijon mustard

½ cup water

1. Heat the oil in a frying pan and brown the brisket on both sides along with the onions.
2. Place the brisket and onions in a crock-pot (slow cooker).
3. Add the water to the pan in which you were frying the meat and scrape up the brown bits stuck to the bottom. Pour this over the meat in the crock-pot.
4. Arrange the potatoes around the meat. I say potatoes are optional, because I sometimes like to serve this dish during the year as a casual light supper on rye bread with mustard and pickles. However, it's also great as a meal served with potatoes and your favourite vegetables.
5. Combine the remaining ingredients in a jug and pour over the meat.
6. Cook on high for 2 hours, then reduce the heat to low and cook for a further 6–8 hours. By then, most of the liquid should have evaporated, leaving behind a lovely glazed, soft brisket. It should be so soft that you hardly need to cut it. You may need two large spoons to get it out of the crock-pot.
7. Place the brisket on a board and shred with a fork. If the strands are a little too long and stringy, cut them shorter.
8. You can add a little more BBQ marinade to the beef at this point if you feel it needs a little more sauce and shine. Warm the BBQ sauce in the microwave or on the stovetop, then pour it over the meat.
9. Serve with the potatoes and a selection of vegetables.

SERVES 8

TOP-RIB FLAPS and onion confit

I love top-rib flaps. My father-in-law, Shmuel, always used to say, 'The closer the bone, the sweeter the meat.' Top-rib flaps are certainly proof of this.

As Rosh Hashanah is the Birthday of Man, here is a cute joke for this time of year.

Q: Why did Adam and Eve have the perfect marriage?

A: He didn't have to hear about all the men she could have married and she didn't have to hear about the way his mother cooked!

So for all those newlyweds, try this before his mom does!

2 tsp coffee powder

1 tsp ground ginger

1 tsp garlic salt

2 Tbsp mushroom or onion soup powder

freshly ground black pepper to taste

2 kg top-rib flaps (you may need 2 as they can be small)

little oil to rub over meat plus a little extra for browning

⅓ cup oil

10 medium onions, peeled and sliced into rings (yes, 10 – it's the caramelised onions
   that take this dish to a new level)

2 bay leaves

1. Preheat the oven to 170 °C. Mix the coffee, ginger, garlic salt, soup powder and black pepper in a small bowl.
2. Using your hands, rub the meat with a little oil and then rub in the coffee and spice mix.
3. Place a little oil in a large deep frying pan or heavy-based saucepan.
4. Brown the meat on both sides and set aside in an ovenproof roasting pan, ensuring that there is room for the 2 pieces to lie side by side and not on top of each other.
5. To the same pan in which you fried the meat, add the ⅓ cup oil and fry the onions until just soft.
6. Place the onions in the same roasting pan as the meat, lifting the meat so that half of the onions are under the meat and half on top of it.
7. Add the bay leaves, cover and place the pan in the oven for 1½ hours.
8. Remove from the oven, stir the onions around and return to the oven, uncovered, for a further 30 minutes.
9. The onions should go a lovely rich, golden colour. If you find they are getting too brown, reduce the heat. If not brown enough, increase the heat a little during the last 30 minutes.
10. Serve with roast or mashed potatoes.

SERVES 6–8

GRANNY SMITH'S raisin' the roof off

This recipe is dedicated to my granny, Gracie Smith (OBM), AKA Granny Smith. Rosh Hashanah is apple and honey time and I couldn't think of a better time to dedicate a recipe to such a sweet person, who even had apples named after her! She loved singing (soprano at that!), especially for her guests after supper. She may not have had the vocals of Sarah Brightman, but she sure had a full house whenever she could. Her hospitality and the guests she entertained always made for an exciting evening, even if it ended on a flat note!

2 Granny Smith apples, peeled and roughly chopped
100 g pitted prunes
1 x 410 g can apricots in syrup (retain juice)
2 Tbsp tomato paste
1 Tbsp cornflour
2 Tbsp soy sauce
2.5–3 kg raisin rib roast
coarsely ground black pepper to taste

1. Preheat the oven to 180 °C.
2. Blend the apples, prunes, apricots, tomato paste, cornflour and soy sauce in a food processor until smooth.
3. Spice the meat well with coarsely ground black pepper.
4. Place the meat in a small, but deep, roasting dish, with about 1 cm spare at either end and round the sides. It should almost fit like a glove!
5. Pour over the sauce, cover with foil and roast for 1½ hours.
6. Then reduce the heat to 170 °C, turn the meat over and continue to roast for 40 minutes uncovered.
7. Turn the meat over again and roast for a further 30–40 minutes, basting every 15 minutes until a rich golden-brown glaze forms around the meat.
8. Serve with your favourite vegetables and potato kugel (see page 30).

SERVES 10–12

sticky ginger-and-honey-**BASTED RIBS**

There are so many different ways to prepare ribs, but this recipe has stood the test of time and comes out tops on every occasion. Remember it's Rosh Hashanah – we need all the sweetness we can get!

3 racks of lamb ribs (about 7 ribs per rack), ask your butcher to cut them up individually (they can be smoked or plain – I prefer them smoked!)
1 litre ginger ale
3 bay leaves
5 whole cloves garlic
1 tsp salt

BASTING SAUCE
2 Tbsp grated fresh ginger
6 cloves garlic, crushed
2 Tbsp treacle sugar
½ cup honey
½ cup soy sauce
2 Tbsp tomato paste
juice of 1 lime
1 tsp salt
1 Tbsp coarsely ground black pepper

1. Place the individually cut ribs in a pot.
2. Combine the ginger ale, bay leaves, garlic and salt and pour over the ribs.
3. Bring to the boil, then reduce the heat and simmer for about 30 minutes, with the lid on, until the liquid boils away.
4. Remove the ribs from the pot and place in a roasting pan.
5. Combine all the basting ingredients in a bowl and pour over the ribs, ensuring that they are completely covered.
6. The ribs can now be either roasted or braaied.
7. If you are going to braai them, braai until golden brown on both sides. They can then be placed in a preheated oven at 140 °C to keep warm. If you are going to roast them, roast for at least 1 hour at 180 °C until brown, turning them after 30 minutes. You can then reduce the heat to 140 °C to keep warm.

SERVES 6–8

pomegranate CHICKEN

I'm always eager to experiment with different tastes and the sudden popularity of pomegranate juice got my taste buds going. In the old days, it was an apple a day that kept the doctor away. Today, it seems that pomegranates are knocking that theory off the tree! To get all of the benefits that pomegranate juice has to offer, keep it healthy and use only fresh ingredients for this recipe.

6–8 thick chicken schnitzels
little oil for frying

MARINADE
2 cups pomegranate juice (I use Goldcrest)
¾ cup low-sodium soy sauce
bunch of fresh coriander, chopped
1 tsp crushed fresh garlic
1 Tbsp grated fresh ginger
1 tsp freshly ground black pepper

1. Rinse the chicken schnitzels and place them in a large Ziploc™ bag.
2. Combine the marinade ingredients in a bowl, mix well and pour over the schnitzels.
3. Place the bag in the fridge to marinate overnight.
4. Next morning, turn the bag over and marinate for a further 12 hours, so that the schnitzels are evenly marinated.
5. The chicken should marinate for no less than 24 hours.
6. Although the marinade makes the schnitzels look very dark, something interesting happens when you cook the meat. The inside becomes white, succulent and tender, with just the outside of the schnitzel retaining that dark caramel colour.
7. Heat a little oil in a frying pan, just enough to coat the bottom.
8. Remove the schnitzels from the marinade, shake off the excess liquid and fry them.
9. Don't put more than three schnitzels in the frying pan at a time, as they will boil rather than fry to a nice golden brown.
10. Fry each schnitzel for 5 minutes on one side, then turn over and fry until cooked through.
11. Be careful not to overcook the schnitzels as they dry out very quickly.
12. Serve immediately with Basmati rice.

SERVES 6–8

tzimmes STUFFED BUTTERNUT

Apparently there are some vegetarians out there! Being a 'meataholic', I find this quite horrifying! I tease my one and only vegetarian friend (only one, I wouldn't allow any more!) that eating a piece of dried mango is no substitute for a piece of biltong! I'm sure she's permanently hungry! Anyway, during the year I make her salads, but on Rosh Hashanah I make her something a little more traditional. For a different way to serve vegetarian tzimmes, try this.

1 large butternut (25–30 cm long)
3 medium potatoes, peeled and cubed
5 medium carrots, peeled and cubed
1 medium sweet potato, peeled and cubed
100 g pitted prunes
1 Tbsp brown sugar
1 tsp salt
¼ tsp ground cinnamon
1 Tbsp preserved ginger syrup (I use Illovo or Sugarbird)
2 tsp cornflour dissolved in ¼ cup cold water

1. Wash the butternut well and, leaving the skin on, cut it in half lengthways. Remove the pips with a spoon and scrape out some of the flesh along the length of the butternut. I scrape out quite a bit so that I can really pack it with the tzimmes.
2. To make the tzimmes, place the cubed potatoes, carrots and sweet potato in a pot and cover with water. If you want to, you can add the butternut that you scraped out (minus the pips!).
3. Bring to the boil, reduce the heat, add the prunes and simmer for 25 minutes.
4. Add the sugar, salt, cinnamon, ginger syrup (I soften the syrup in the microwave first) and cornflour mixture.
5. Stir gently until it thickens, then remove from the heat. Place the lid on the pot and set aside to cool.
6. Preheat the oven to 180 °C.
7. Place both halves of the butternut, cavities facing up, on a lightly oiled piece of thick foil (large enough to wrap the whole butternut in).
8. Fill both butternut halves with the tzimmes, keeping it in line with the rim of the butternut.
9. Using both hands, gently push the two halves of the butternut together, re-forming the whole butternut. Wrap it tightly in the foil.
10. Bake for 1 hour, then reduce the oven temperature to 160 °C and bake for a further 40–45 minutes, or until the butternut is soft and the skin is golden brown. Open the foil, separate the butternut halves and bake a little longer until the tops start to go brown.

SERVES 10–12

coco-peach PUDDING

The secret to this pudding is the size of the baking dish. It shouldn't be less than 35 x 25 cm and shouldn't be deep. If it's too small and deep, the pudding becomes stodgy, rather than light and cakey.

1 x 825 g can peach halves in syrup, drained (syrup reserved) and sliced
1 x 400 ml can coconut milk
1 x 600 g box vanilla cake mix

1. Preheat the oven to 170 °C.
2. Place the drained peaches in a lightly greased ovenproof dish. Retain the syrup.
3. Combine the syrup from the peaches with the coconut milk in a bowl.
4. Add the cake mix to the syrup and milk mixture and mix well. Pour the mixture over the peaches.
5. Bake for 50 minutes and serve with pareve custard (see page 134).

SERVES 10–12

and its cousin … PINA COLADA BEACH TRIFLE

1 x 600 g box vanilla cake mix
1 cup coconut milk
1 x 440 g can crushed pineapple in syrup
1 x 90 g pkt pineapple jelly dissolved in 2 cups warm water

1 cup non-dairy creamer
1 x 90 g box vanilla instant pudding
1 cup soy or coconut milk
desiccated coconut to serve

1. Preheat the oven and bake the cake according to the instructions on the box, but substitute the milk with coconut milk. Bake it in a round cake tin, about 20–22 cm in diameter.
2. Meanwhile, combine the crushed pineapple and dissolved pineapple jelly in a saucepan and bring to the boil. Remove from the heat and set aside to cool.
3. Beat the non-dairy creamer until firm and set aside.
4. In a separate bowl, beat the vanilla pudding with the soy or coconut milk using an electric beater. Once well incorporated and smooth, reduce the speed and mix in the firmly beaten creamer. Place in the fridge.
5. When the cake is ready, remove from the oven and cool. Once cool, cut the cake horizontally into three layers. Don't worry if it crumbles, as the layers can be crumbled into the trifle bowl.
6. Place a layer of the pineapple mixture in a large glass trifle bowl, followed by a layer of sponge and a layer of creamer mixture. Repeat the layers, ending with a layer of creamer mixture. More layers look prettier and keep the sponge more moist.
7. Toast the desiccated coconut in a hot oven until golden brown (watch as it can burn quickly). Sprinkle on top of the trifle just before serving.

SERVES 10–12

Pina Colada beach trifle

quick and easy PAREVE CUSTARD

2 Tbsp custard powder
2 Tbsp sugar
1 cup soy milk
1 cup non-dairy creamer
1 vanilla pod or 1 tsp vanilla essence

1. Dissolve the custard powder and sugar in the cold soy milk in a saucepan.
2. Add the non-dairy creamer and whisk until well combined.
3. Add the vanilla pod or essence.
4. Place on the stove over a medium to high heat and keep stirring until it thickens.
5. Remove from the heat and allow to absorb all the flavours for about 30 minutes.
6. When ready to serve, reheat and then remove the vanilla pod if used. It can also be served at room temperature.

SINNA'S APPLE SAUCE and raisin muffins

My mother-in-law's domestic helper, Sinna, is a wonderful baker. When I get that muffin craving she gets out the raisins and whips up her wonderful muffins in no time. They freeze very well, although we don't really give them the opportunity to be frozen, because they stay moist for four to five days in a plastic bag. They make the best Rosh Hashanah breakfast treat!

4 eggs
2 cups white sugar
1½ cups oil
1¾ cups apple sauce
3 cups cake flour
1 Tbsp ground cinnamon
2 tsp baking powder
2 tsp bicarbonate of soda
1 tsp salt
2 cups raisins
brown sugar for sprinkling

1. Preheat the oven to 190 °C.
2. In a large mixing bowl, lightly beat the eggs and add the sugar, oil and apple sauce. Beat thoroughly.
3. Add the dry ingredients and blend until smooth.
4. Stir in the raisins.
5. Spoon the batter into greased muffin tins, filling them three-quarters full, and sprinkle brown sugar on top.
6. Bake for 15–20 minutes.

MAKES 18

ROSH HASHANAH PUDDING

Just in case apple sorbet doesn't do it for you!

1½ cups cake flour, sifted

1 cup treacle sugar

2 tsp ground ginger

1 tsp ground allspice

2 tsp baking powder

1 cup soy milk

½ cup oil

2 eggs, lightly beaten

1 cup raisins

SAUCE

½ cup treacle sugar

1 tsp ground ginger

1 tsp ground mixed spice

2 heaped Tbsp margarine

1 cup boiling water

1. Preheat the oven to 180 °C.
2. Combine the flour, treacle sugar, ginger, mixed spice and baking powder in a large mixing bowl.
3. Make a well in the centre and pour in the soy milk, oil and eggs.
4. Mix with a wooden spoon, before adding the raisins. Stir well.
5. Pour into a fairly deep, lightly greased pie dish and set aside.
6. To make the sauce, place the treacle sugar, ginger, mixed spice and margarine into a bowl, then add the boiling water. Mix until dissolved.
7. Pour the hot sauce over the raw cake batter and bake for 45 minutes. A metal skewer won't come out clean, as this is a moist pudding.
8. Serve with vanilla ice cream and 'To-Crown-It-All' Peaches (page 221).

SERVES 8

apple SORBET

One of the most wonderful birthday presents I ever received was a three-day stay at Singita Ebony lodge, situated in the Sabi Sands Game Reserve. I travel everywhere with a set of Egyptian cotton sheets, 'obsessive' behaviour for which I'm notorious! However, this is the only place in the world that I haven't had to take my linen out of the suitcase! Naturally, I was drawn to the kitchen and, in no time, the executive chef, Kyle, was sharing his apple sorbet recipe with me. This fresh sorbet is all one really needs after a Yomtov meal. However, on Rosh Hashanah, a platter of Parisienne Pinwheels (page 139), Almond and Cranberry Biscotti (below) and Pareve Chocolate Fudge (page 140) goes down well too.

2 Granny Smith apples, peeled, cored and quartered	½ cup icing sugar
1 cup water	1 litre apple juice

1. Boil the apples in a saucepan with the water and icing sugar. Once the apples are soft, remove the pan from the heat and blend with a hand blender or in a food processor. Add the apple juice and mix well. If you want it to look a little greener, then add 1 drop of green food colouring and mix very well.
2. Pour the mixture through a strainer into a rectangular container and freeze for 6 hours.
3. Remove from the freezer and rake the sorbet with a fork, mixing it up well. Alternatively, scoop it out and blend in a food processor until smooth. Raking it makes it more like a granita, whereas blending it while almost frozen makes it more velvety and smooth. Refreeze.
4. Remove from the freezer about 10 minutes before serving to soften it a little.

SERVES 12

almond and cranberry BISCOTTI

Or mandelbrodt *in our language!*

1 cup sugar	1½–2 cups self-raising flour
⅓ cup non-dairy margarine	½ cup almond nibs or chopped pistachios
2 eggs	3 Tbsp dried cranberries
1 tsp vanilla essence	

1. Preheat the oven to 180 °C.
2. In a mixing bowl, cream the sugar and margarine. Add the eggs and vanilla essence and mix well.
3. Stir in the flour, almonds or pistachios and cranberries.
4. On a floured surface, roll the dough into a sausage shape. Place on a baking tray and bake for 20 minutes.
5. Remove from the oven and allow to cool for 15 minutes – no longer, as it becomes too hard to cut. If you're like me and forget, just return it to the oven for a few minutes and it will soften again.
6. Cut into 2 cm-thick slices and lay them flat on the baking tray.
7. Bake for a further 15 minutes, then turn off the heat, turn over the cookies and leave in the oven for 10 minutes.

MAKES ABOUT 30

Apple sorbet

PARISIENNE pinwheels

At this time of year, sorbet, ice cream and fresh fruit are definitely the flavours of the month. These, served with platters of light, delicate smalls such as Teiglach, are guaranteed to do the dessert trick. You can double-up on this recipe as they keep well in an airtight container or in the freezer. Almonds can be replaced with 1 cup roughly chopped dates and pistachio nuts replaced with 100 g chocolate chips.

1 cup treacle sugar
1 Tbsp ground cinnamon
100 g flaked almonds, crushed slightly with the back of a spoon
100 g chopped almonds
1 x 500 g pkt (8 sheets) phyllo pastry
olive oil, for spraying/brushing
1 kg golden syrup (rather have too much than too little, as you really need to drench them!)
100 g pistachio nuts, lightly crushed

1. Preheat the oven to 160 °C.
2. In a bowl, combine the treacle sugar, cinnamon and both kinds of almonds.
3. Spray 4 sheets of the phyllo pastry with olive oil spray (or lightly brush with olive oil) and stack them one on top of the other.
4. Sprinkle the top layer with half of the almond mixture.
5. Warm the syrup in the microwave or on the stovetop and drizzle ¼–½ cup over the nuts.
6. Fold in the sides of the phyllo pastry (2 cm on each side) and roll up all 4 sheets as you would a Swiss roll.
7. Repeat with the remaining 4 sheets of phyllo pastry.
8. Line a baking tray with a layer of baking paper.
9. Cut the rolls into 1–2 cm slices and lay each 'pinwheel' flat on the lined baking tray so that you can see the spiral pattern.
10. Spray them with olive oil spray (or lightly brush with olive oil), then sprinkle over the lightly crushed pistachio nuts.
11. Bake for 20–25 minutes until golden brown. Baking them on a lower heat for a longer period ensures that they will be crisp all the way through.
12. If they aren't golden brown, leave them in for a little longer.
13. As they come out of the oven, drizzle with a little more syrup so that they are comfortably soaked.

MAKES 30–40

lekker HONEY CAKE

Honey cake, traditionally served on Rosh Hashanah to symbolise a sweet year, is called lekach *in Yiddish. Being South African, I just had to call it* lekker, *meaning 'nice, really nice'! What could be better than a sweet,* lekker *year?*

4 eggs	½ tsp bicarbonate of soda dissolved in
1 cup brown sugar	¾ cup apple juice
1 cup honey or golden syrup	½ tsp ground cinnamon
1 cup oil	1 tsp ground ginger
2 cups sifted cake flour	pinch of salt
	1½ tsp baking powder

1. Preheat the oven to 180 °C.
2. In a mixing bowl, cream the eggs and sugar.
3. Add the honey or syrup and oil, and continue to beat for about 1 minute.
4. Slowly add the flour, a cup at a time, alternating with the apple juice mixture.
5. Add the cinnamon, ginger, salt and baking powder.
6. Pour the batter into 2 greased, medium-sized loaf tins and bake for 45–50 minutes. The cake is done when a metal skewer inserted into the centre comes out clean.

pareve (non-dairy) CHOCOLATE FUDGE

I made this for my 50th birthday party and, when it came to serving the desserts, I couldn't find it! Non-dairy fudge is something special and I knew I had made it, or maybe I imagined I had! Ageing isn't easy! At the end of the evening I see the back end of somebody on the floor with his head under the table. Sure enough, my cousin had hidden the fudge to eat on the plane on his way back to Australia! So for my poor friends who didn't get a piece, here's the recipe!

2 x 250 ml boxes Orley Whip™ Non-dairy Cream

3 cups sugar

1 vanilla pod

¼ cup Cardin margarine

¼ cup cocoa or 150 g pareve chocolate

1. Place the Orley Whip™ in a heavy-based saucepan, followed by the sugar and vanilla pod.
2. Stirring continuously with a whisk, bring to the boil over a high heat. As it starts to boil, reduce the heat to a 'slower' boil and and keep stirring with your whisk for 20–25 minutes, until it starts to reduce and thicken.
3. Remove from the heat, remove the vanilla pod, add the margarine and cocoa or chocolate and stir.
4. At this point, you may find it has crystallised too much. Add 1 x 125 ml sachet of Orley Whip™ and return to the heat to combine. It will become smooth again.
5. Pour the mixture onto a baking tray, allow to set, then cut into squares and enjoy!

MAKES A BAKING-TRAY FULL

YOM KIPPUR

Writing this, I couldn't believe how (*dafkeh* while talking about a fast day) my mind kept wandering off in the direction of food! Nothing too exciting at first, just the thought of kreplach and bland chicken to start the fast, but then warm bulkes and cheesecake to break it felt a little more comforting. I shouldn't compare the two, I know, because after 25 hours of fasting, boiled chicken can also start to sound good!

My kitchen isn't really '*milchik* friendly' and my family like to break their fasts on *milchiks* (dairy), so my sister-in-law Loren always hosts the breaking of the fast. We let her off just once, to have my twin nieces Ella and Scarlett, who were born on Yom Kippur's day! But she resumed office the following year.

We start the fast with a festive meal just before sunset and traditionally serve chicken soup (page 23) and kreplach (page 214), followed by roast chicken and vegetables. Just because we are fasting doesn't mean the chicken has to be tasteless and look pale and *milchik*. Such unappetising memories we don't have to pass on to our children! A simple trick to prevent this is to use a vertical roaster. A vertical roaster is a metal stand that is used to stand a chicken upright while roasting in the oven. It makes the chicken nice and crisp with a lovely golden-brown colour. Place the chicken upright on a vertical roaster, making sure the top of the roaster pokes through the neck cavity. If you don't have a vertical roaster you can use an empty cooldrink can.

Rub the chicken with a little oil and sprinkle lightly with your favourite herbs and spices (more herbs than spices, as you don't want to be too thirsty during the fast). I like to tuck fresh herbs, like rosemary, under the skin of the chicken so that the flavours permeate through the meat. Roast at 180 °C for 1½ hours.

We like to end our meal with apple tzimmes (stewed apples), fresh fruit salad and a little jelly. I know it may sound a bit like hospital food, but everybody can do with a little healing at this time of the year!

Although Yom Kippur (Day of Atonement) is a day for repenting, we should nevertheless feel a certain amount of confidence that G-d will forgive us and bless us all (PG) with another year of life, love and laughter.

SUKKOT

SUKKOT

Sukkot, another one of my favourite holidays … okay, let's just say I love them all … gets its name from the very structures in which we eat for eight days – *sukkot* (huts or booths).

Until the culmination of the holiday with Simchas Torah, we eat every meal in our *sukkah*. At Simchas Torah we have an absolute blast as we celebrate our never-ending dedication to the study of Torah. The Torah is divided into portions that are read on a weekly basis. On Simchas Torah, the last portion of the Torah is read and, since we never finish reading the Torah, we immediately begin reading from the very beginning again so that the cycle of Torah reading and learning never ends.

Children receive chocolates and flags on Simchas Torah and the festive atmosphere really draws the crowds.

Growing up in Durban had its advantages, especially at this time of the year, as a member of our shul owned Beacon Sweets and he would donate specially made boxes of sweets to our community. But that wasn't all; we had a little '*Protecsia*', because part of being on the shul's committee included my father having 'sole distribution rights' for the sweets! I certainly wouldn't have taken on the job. You try and tell Mrs Cohen that she can't have eight boxes for her grandchildren living in Toronto!

This section is rather large as I have tried to include a different meal option for each night of Sukkot. Obviously one can take any recipe in the book and include it in any of the Sukkot meals. We need to eat quite a few meals in the *sukkah* and many of the Shabbat salads and Rosh Hashanah meals would also go down well. Nothing wrong with pick-and-mix!

dream of TOMATO SOUP

It was a hectic week. I'd been cooking for Yomtov, broken my arm, had deadlines for articles and, the biggest headache of all: THE SEARCH FOR MY DAUGHTER EDEN'S DANCE DRESS! Anything that didn't look good was naturally my fault: Why did she have to get my swimming shoulders when she doesn't even swim? Why did she have to be as tall as me? Perhaps what she should have asked was why they make dresses so damn short these days! We schlepped from one side of Gauteng to the other and if there had been a sea in the middle I may just have driven into it! Just dreaming about a bowl of hot, homemade tomato soup when I got home kept me going!

little oil for roasting and frying

18 fresh Italian jam tomatoes (not canned, as you need the skins for the smoky flavour and darker colouring)

3 large red peppers, deseeded and quartered

½ cup brown sugar

salt to taste

4 large onions, peeled and chopped

4 celery sticks, chopped

35 g fresh basil, chopped

1 heaped tsp hot chilli sauce (see page 25)

1 tsp crushed fresh garlic

5 cups water

1 x 115 g can tomato paste

2 heaped Tbsp chicken stock powder

2 heaped Tbsp onion soup powder

2 cups Orley Whip™ Cook 'n Crème

salt and freshly ground black pepper to taste

1. Place a little oil in a large baking tray.
2. Cut the tops off the tomatoes, then cut the tomatoes in half.
3. Place the flat side of the tomatoes on a baking tray and add the quartered peppers.
4. Sprinkle with the brown sugar and a little salt.
5. Place the baking tray in the upper third of the oven under the griller and grill until the tomatoes and peppers are dark brown and their skins are able to peel off easily.
6. Heat a little oil in a large soup pot and fry the onions until golden brown.
7. Add the celery, basil, chilli sauce and garlic and continue to cook until limp.
8. Add 3 cups of the water and bring to the boil. Once boiling, reduce the heat and allow to simmer.
9. When all the tomatoes and peppers are cooked and their skins removed, add them, together with the juice they made, to the pot.
10. Add the remaining 2 cups of water, the tomato paste and stock powders and bring to the boil.
11. Reduce the heat and simmer for about 2 hours.
12. Using a hand blender, blend the soup until smooth.
13. Add the Orley Whip™ and continue to blend well until smooth. If you feel the soup is a bit too thick, add a little hot water and a little more stock powder.
14. Season with salt and pepper according to taste.

SERVES 10–12

fresh carrot and corn SOUP

Carrots are a goldmine of nutrients. For the best taste results, use fresh all the way. You want bright orange carrots, with feathery green ponytails, which seem such a pity to discard, and mealies bulging with perfect rows of teeth that you slice off the cob. Now that's what I call fresh! Believe me, you'll taste the difference between that and anything frozen or precut.

little oil for frying
2 onions, peeled and roughly chopped
1 Tbsp grated fresh ginger
1 heaped tsp ground cumin
1 tsp curry powder
1 kg carrots, peeled and cut into 2 cm pieces
1 kg corn (off the cob)
1 litre water (you may need a little more as some soup pots are bigger than others,
   causing liquid to evaporate quicker)
1 litre Nussbaums chicken soup or homemade chicken stock (or 3 chicken stock cubes
   dissolved in 1 litre water)
salt and pepper to taste

1. Heat the oil in a large soup pot and fry the onions and ginger until the onions become glassy.
2. Add the cumin and curry powder and fry for 1 minute.
3. Add the carrots, two-thirds of the corn (about 650 g), the water and soup or stock.
4. Bring to the boil, reduce the heat and simmer, covered, for 1½ hours.
5. Meanwhile, fry the remaining corn in a little oil in a frying pan until golden brown. Set aside to cool.
6. After 1½ hours, remove the soup from the heat and liquidise it, either in a food processor or with a hand blender. If you feel the soup is too thick, add a little more stock or water. You don't want it to be too smooth; just nicely blended with a grainy texture.
7. Season with salt and pepper. The carrots and corn are rather sweet, so you will need salt to bring out the other flavours in the soup.
8. Return the soup to the pot to reheat before serving with the fried corn sprinkled on top.

SERVES 8–10

TUSCAN beef ribs

Don't you just love the look on a person's face when they taste something really delicious and can't help showing it? The first mouthful really says it all. Hopefully it doesn't go under the gem-squash shell!

Well, this fast way of cooking slowly really allows one to experience a fusion of fresh tastes. Put it on in the morning and by suppertime you have a tasty, flavourful meal that on first mouthful proves me right.

2.5 kg short ribs (ask your butcher to use top ribs as they're
   meatier and to slice them horizontally into 3 cm strips)
salt and pepper to taste
little oil for frying
2 large onions, peeled and chopped
6 cloves garlic, crushed
bunch of fresh parsley, chopped
35 g fresh basil, chopped
1 x 410 g can chopped peeled tomatoes
1 x 115 g can tomato paste
1 heaped tsp brown sugar
1½ cups red wine or beef stock
2 bay leaves
2 x 285g cans sliced mushrooms

1. Lightly spice the ribs with salt and pepper then fry them in a frying pan with a little oil until golden brown. This is important, as you not only want them to be golden brown in colour, but you need to deglaze the pan and use that liquid to cook the ribs in the crock-pot (slow cooker).
2. Once brown, place the ribs in a crock-pot.
3. Add a little oil to the pan you've just used and fry the onions and garlic. Once lightly browned, add the parsley, basil, tomatoes, tomato paste, sugar and wine or stock and bring to the boil. Scrape all the dark bits off the bottom of the pan. Reduce the heat and simmer for about 5 minutes.
4. Remove from the heat and pour over the ribs in the crock-pot.
5. Add the bay leaves and mushrooms (with their liquid) and cook the lot on low heat for about 8 hours.
6. Serve with polenta chips (see page 150).

SERVES 6–8

POLENTA CHIPS with rustic vegetables

This is a great dish for people who are gluten intolerant and for those who, like me, can eat anything!

1 x 500 g pkt polenta (I use Pouyoukas)
little salt for sprinkling

RUSTIC VEGETABLES
olive oil for frying
1 onion, peeled and cut in half then sliced into half rings
½ tsp crushed fresh garlic
250 g mushrooms, sliced
8 baby marrows, sliced into rings
1 x 400 g can Italian tomatoes
2 tsp sugar
2 Tbsp Balsamic vinegar
crushed black pepper to taste

1. To make the polenta, follow the cooking instructions on the packet. While still hot, pour the polenta into a baking pan. Sprinkle with a little salt and set aside to cool. Your job's not over yet!
2. You can start making up the vegetables or they can be prepared the day before and just reheated. In fact, I like them done the day before.
3. Heat the oil in a frying pan and fry the onion and garlic until soft.
4. Add the mushrooms and baby marrows and continue to fry until soft.
5. Add the tomatoes, sugar, vinegar and pepper.
6. Bring to the boil, then reduce the heat and simmer for about 5 minutes.
7. When ready to make the polenta chips, preheat the oven to 190 °C.
8. By now the polenta should be cool. Cut it into any shape you desire: diamonds, squares or rectangles are great.
9. Place them on a well-oiled baking tray and bake for about 10 minutes each side, until golden brown.
10. Remove from the oven and serve the chips either on top of or underneath the warmed vegetables.

SERVES 8–10

win him over CABBAGE BLINTZES

Cabbage blintzes (mince meat in cabbage leaves) are one of my husband's favourites, so if I want a new pair of shoes, I make them for him the night before I plan to go shopping!

You'd actually be amazed how many people love mince meat in cabbage leaves. From the very young to the not-so-very young!

1 medium cabbage
1 kg beef mince
2 onions, peeled, chopped and fried
2 Tbsp chopped fresh parsley or
1 tsp dried
½ tsp garlic powder
½ cup cornflake crumbs (you can use matzo meal to make it *Pesachdik*)
½ cup cold water
1 tsp salt

TOMATO SAUCE

8–10 red jam tomatoes, peeled (drop them into boiling water to help remove their skins) and seeded, or 2 x 410 g cans good-quality chopped peeled Italian tomatoes
1 Tbsp cornflour
juice of 1 small lemon (about ¼ cup)
2 Tbsp sugar
2 Tbsp golden syrup
1 heaped tsp finely grated ginger or ¼ tsp ground ginger
1 chicken stock cube dissolved in ½ cup water (left over from boiling cabbage)

1. Bring a large pot of salted water to the boil.
2. Very carefully remove the hard core from the base of the cabbage with a sharp knife. Push the knife about 6 cm down and work around the core to remove it.
3. Remove the leaves, wash them well and place in the pot of boiling water.
4. Cook until tender, about 4–5 minutes. (Don't throw the cabbage water away as you will need some later for the tomato sauce.)
5. While boiling the cabbage, combine the raw mince, fried onions, parsley, garlic powder, cornflake crumbs, water and salt in a large bowl and set aside.
6. Drain the cabbage leaves and allow to cool. (Retain ½ cup of the liquid to mix with the stock cube.)
7. In the meantime, make the tomato sauce by combining all the ingredients and mixing until well blended. You can use a food processor or a hand blender for this.
8. Preheat the oven to 180 °C.
9. Using your hands, roll the mince mixture into balls a bit bigger than golf balls.
10. Take a cabbage leaf and remove the hard vein from the surface with a knife or just roll over it with a rolling pin to soften it.
11. Place a mince ball in the middle of the leaf, fold the sides of the cabbage leaf over the mince meat and roll it up. Don't worry if the leaves aren't perfect; 'patch jobs' work just as well! Repeat until all the mince balls are used up.
12. Place the blintzes in an ovenproof dish, pour over the tomato sauce and cover with a lid or foil.
13. Bake for 30 minutes, then uncover and bake for a further 30–40 minutes or until golden brown.

MAKES 12–14

asparagus CHICKEN

It's amazing how some things stick in your mind and never leave. As children, my brothers and I were never allowed to order asparagus at a restaurant. In the old days, although a delicacy, asparagus as a starter was always the canned version with a blob of mayonnaise and a sprinkle of paprika. My father always said that asparagus was something you ate at home where you could eat the whole can at an eighth of the price. It was a 'blatant waste of money and an unnecessary extravagance' – soup, on the other hand, at double the price, was fine!

Sukkot time is a good month in South Africa for fresh asparagus – so 'Ess gezunterheydt' – but keep it fresh, not canned!

6 thick thigh chicken schnitzels, cut into 3 or 4 strips
salt and pepper to taste
⅓ cup cake flour or cornflour (for dusting)
little oil for frying
500 g fresh asparagus, chopped into 1 cm pieces
1 cup non-dairy creamer
1 cup soy milk
1 heaped Tbsp chicken stock powder
1 heaped Tbsp cornflour
1 tsp mustard powder
1 tsp mustard seeds
1 tsp ground turmeric
1 tsp paprika

1. Preheat the oven to 180 °C.
2. Sprinkle the chicken strips with salt and pepper and coat with the flour or cornflour.
3. Fry the chicken strips in a little hot oil until golden brown all over. Place the browned strips in an ovenproof dish and set aside.
4. Place the asparagus in a saucepan, cover with boiling water from the kettle and allow to stand for 3–4 minutes. Drain and set aside.
5. In a bowl, combine the non-dairy creamer, soy milk, chicken stock powder, cornflour, mustard powder, mustard seeds, turmeric and paprika.
6. Bring to the boil in a saucepan on the stove, whisking all the while.
7. Once it starts to thicken, reduce the heat and simmer for another 1–2 minutes.
8. Remove from the heat, add the asparagus and pour over the chicken.
9. Bake in the oven for 25–30 minutes until bubbling.
10. Serve with baby potatoes and minted peas.

SERVES 5–6

KUNG PAO chicken

There was a man named Dan,
Who knew my sister-in-law De Anne.
Kung Pao chicken was his best,
And to that she will attest.
Hence her favourite take-away,
Which she gets every day!

1 hot chilli, finely chopped, or 2 tsp
hot chilli sauce (see page 25)
2 tsp finely grated fresh ginger
6 spring onions, chopped (put 2 Tbsp
aside for sprinkling at the end)
little oil for frying
½ tsp crushed garlic
2 Tbsp soy sauce
1 Tbsp red wine vinegar
1 heaped Tbsp brown sugar

1 level tsp peanut butter
1 Tbsp cornflour dissolved in 1 cup
cold water
2 egg whites
4 Tbsp soy sauce
2 Tbsp cornflour
1 kg chicken schnitzels, cut into 2.5 cm
strips 'shwarma-style'
oil for deep-frying
1 cup raw peanuts or cashew nuts

1. Fry the chilli, ginger and spring onions in a little oil in a frying pan until soft.
2. Remove from the heat and add the garlic, soy sauce, vinegar, sugar and peanut butter, stirring well after each addition.
3. Return to the heat and add the dissolved cornflour, stirring as you do so, until the sauce starts to thicken. Once it starts to thicken, remove from the heat and set aside.
4. Meanwhile, combine the egg whites, soy sauce and cornflour in a shallow dish.
5. Lightly coat the chicken strips in the egg white mixture.
6. Heat the oil (enough to reach about 2.5 cm up the sides of the frying pan) and deep-fry a few strips at a time. Drain on an absorbent paper towel and set aside.
7. When all the chicken is fried, place in a serving bowl.
8. Bring the sauce to the boil again, then remove from the heat, pour over the chicken and gently mix to ensure that all pieces are evenly coated.
9. Sprinkle with the peanuts or cashew nuts and the remaining chopped spring onion and serve immediately on a bed of rice.

TIP: While frying the chicken, preheat the oven to 220 °C. Place the nuts on a baking tray on the middle rack of the oven and roast until lightly browned. Alternatively, dry-fry them in an ungreased frying pan or oven grill them. This gives the nuts an added crunch.

SERVES 4–5

BOLLYWOOD beef

This dish can be as colourful in flavour as a Bollywood movie or as fiery and spicy as an X-rated film! One thing is guaranteed – it will spice up your life for sure!

1 kg beef, cut stroganoff-style
little cornflour for coating
¼ cup peri oil (I use Debras)
1 red onion, peeled and chopped
1 tsp crushed garlic
2 bird's-eye chillies, chopped, or 2 tsp dried chilli flakes
1 thumb-size knob of grated fresh ginger
2 Tbsp finely grated fresh coriander
1 tsp ground cumin
2 tsp paprika
2–3 cardamom pods
1 cinnamon stick
3 ripe tomatoes, finely chopped
1 tsp sugar
2 Tbsp tomato paste
½ cup coconut milk
salt and freshly ground black pepper to taste

1. Preheat the oven to 180 °C.
2. Place the meat in a bowl and sift over a little cornflour. Mix well to coat.
3. Fry the meat in the peri oil in a frying pan, in small batches so that it browns quickly.
4. Remove from the pan and set aside in an ovenproof dish.
5. In the same pan, add a little more peri oil and fry the onion, garlic, chillies, ginger and coriander for about 1 minute.
6. Add the cumin, paprika, cardamom pods and cinnamon stick and give it a good stir.
7. Add the tomatoes, sugar, tomato paste, coconut milk, salt and pepper and continue to stir until it starts to boil.
8. Once boiling, remove from the heat and pour over the meat.
9. Cover and bake in the oven for 35–40 minutes.
10. Remove the cardamom pods and cinnamon stick just before serving. Serve on a bed of Basmati rice with a side serving of chutney.

SERVES 4–5

cubed steak À LA RYAN

I feel sorry for my son Ryan's future wife (PG). He is the fussiest, most fastidious, finicky eater around! If he sees a thread of fat in his meat, he 'politely' lifts his eyebrows and sighs like a willow wafting in the wind!

However, this recipe may cause him to turn a blind sigh!

1.5 kg Scotch fillet, cut into 3 cm cubes (little larger than normal)
little oil for frying

MARINADE
1 Tbsp crushed peppercorns
3 cm piece fresh ginger, grated
⅓ cup soy sauce
½ tsp crushed garlic
½ cup sunflower oil

WARM DRESSING
1 cup rice vinegar
175 g castor sugar
2 Tbsp soy sauce
35 g fresh coriander, chopped

1. Place the cubed beef in a Ziploc™ bag.
2. Combine the marinade ingredients in a bowl and pour over the cubed beef. Allow to marinate for 24 hours.
3. To make the dressing, bring the vinegar and castor sugar to the boil in a small saucepan, then reduce the heat and simmer for about 10 minutes. Remove from the heat, add the soy sauce and coriander and allow to cool. Refrigerate and reheat when ready to serve.
4. When ready to cook, remove the meat from the bag and fry in a little oil over a high heat until golden brown. Don't overcook. First prize would be to braai the beef cubes on a gas barbecue, but if that is not an option then frying them on the stove is just as acceptable.
5. Once cooked, place the beef cubes in a serving dish and drizzle over the warm dressing. Alternatively, thread the cubes onto wooden skewers, alternating with some sliced red onion, green pepper and halved cherry tomatoes.

SERVES 4–6

chilli CON CARNE

Whenever I make this dish I can't help thinking of that famous scene from Mel Brooks' movie Blazing Saddles *where they're all sitting around the fire, eating their beans and experiencing the side effects thereof. I don't know if it's the beans in the dish, the tin plates I like to serve it on, or that they were eating under open skies that makes me want to tie this meal up with Sukkot. Whatever the reason, if you feel like a good laugh, rent the movie!*

¼ cup oil	1 x 65 g can tomato paste
1 large onion, peeled and chopped	1 tsp sugar
1 green pepper, deseeded and chopped	1 tsp salt
2 carrots, peeled and grated	1 x 410 g can baked beans in tomato sauce
1 heaped tsp crushed garlic	½ tsp paprika
1 kg beef mince	1 tsp hot chilli sauce (see page 25) or
½ cup cold water	½ tsp chilli powder
2 x 410 g cans chopped peeled tomatoes	pinch of ground cinnamon

1. Heat the oil in a large frying pan and sauté the onion, green pepper, carrots and garlic.
2. Remove from the pan and set aside.
3. In the same pan, fry the mince with the water. The water helps to separate the mince to prevent clumps from forming.
4. Add the remaining ingredients, along with the sautéed vegetables, and simmer on a low heat for 40–45 minutes.

SERVES 8–10

On a recent visit to New York, I had the pleasure of 'meating' chefs from some of the best kosher restaurants around. The best part, of course, was peeping into the holding fridges, where some meat is dry-aged for 60 days! In the whole-rib sections, which house the prime cuts, carcasses are aged in one piece and the restaurants have their own band saws, which they use to cut the meat themselves.

I was only in Manhattan for 48 hours and about 30 of them were devoted to meat. Two of my most memorable experiences were 'meating' up with David Kolotkin of the Prime Grill and Solo restaurants and Jeff Nathan of Abigail's Restaurant, both of whom hold very high standards in excellent cuisine. Here I share two wonderful recipes from them.

JEFF NATHAN'S BRAISED BEEF with dried fruits and port wine sauce

1.8 kg boneless top rib cut into
3 cm strips
kosher salt and freshly ground
black pepper
little vegetable oil
¾ cup dried fruit (cherries,
apricots, cranberries)
2 Tbsp light brown sugar
2 cups red wine
1¼ cup port wine or Kiddush wine
4 medium red onions, peeled and
sliced into half moons

1 medium white onion, peeled and
sliced into half moons
1 large leek, white part only, washed
and sliced into half moons
1 cup beef stock
2 bay leaves
1 tsp dried thyme
12 whole black peppercorns
1 bunch of parsley stems, leaves
reserved and chopped
2 Tbsp cornflour

1. Preheat the oven to 150 °C.
2. Season the meat with the salt and pepper. Heat the oil in a large ovenproof skillet/frying pan. In batches, sear the meat on all sides. Do not overcrowd the pan. Reserve the seared meat.
3. While the meat is being seared, combine the dried fruit with the sugar, red wine and 1 cup of the port wine in a small bowl. Set aside.
4. Add the onions and leek to the skillet and cook, stirring occasionally, for 5 minutes. Pour in the dried fruit with the wines and the beef stock. Transfer the meat back to the skillet.
5. In a 20 cm-square, double layer of cheesecloth, tie up the bay leaves, thyme, peppercorns and parsley stems. Submerge this sachet in the liquid of the skillet. Bring the liquid up to a simmer and then transfer everything to an ovenproof roasting dish. Cover and place in the oven to cook until tender, 1½–2 hours.
6. Remove the meat from the roasting dish and keep warm. Remove and discard the muslin sachet. Pour the liquid into a saucepan on the stovetop and bring it to a simmer.
7. In a small bowl, combine the cornflour with the remaining port wine. Whisk this into the simmering liquid. Simmer for 5 more minutes.
8. Place the meat back in the sauce and stir in the chopped parsley. Serve hot.

SERVES 6–8

DAVID KOLOTKIN'S rack of lamb

Mustard-crusted rack of lamb, celery root purée, caramelised onions and fried rosemary. Yum!

6 x 3-bone racks of lamb, French trimmed
salt and pepper to taste
1 Tbsp oil
2 medium onions, peeled and sliced into rings
1 tsp brown sugar
½ cup water
salt to taste
2 Tbsp chopped parsley
1 Tbsp chopped rosemary
1 cup cornflake crumbs or Japanese breadcrumbs if available
½ cup ready prepared Dijon mustard paste
8–10 sprigs of rosemary fried in hot oil until crispy for decoration

CELERY ROOT PURÉE

1 celery root* (round celeriac bulb, you may need 2), peeled and diced small
3 cups water
2 cups non-dairy creamer (I use Orley Whip™ Cook 'n Crème)
salt and pepper to taste
100 g non-dairy margarine

*Celery root is the big root bulb at the end of celery sticks, about the size of gem squash. In America they are double that size, which is why I have said two in this recipe. If you can't find celery root, then turnips also work well.

1. Preheat the oven to 180 °C.
2. Dry the lamb with a paper towel and season with salt and pepper.
3. Heat the oil in a sauté pan and brown the lamb over a high heat on both sides. Remove from the pan and wrap the bones (not the meat) in foil.
4. To the same pan in which the lamb was fried, add a little more oil and fry the onions until dark brown. When they start turning brown, add the brown sugar and continue to fry until the sugar dissolves. Add the water and a little salt and bring to the boil. Then reduce the heat and simmer for about 10 minutes until most of the liquid has evaporated. Set aside.
5. Mix the chopped parsley, chopped rosemary and crumbs in a bowl.
6. Brush the lamb on the top side with the mustard and dredge in the herb and crumb mixture.
7. Roast in the oven for 20–25 minutes until medium rare. (My family prefer it a little more well done, so I turned the oven down to 160 °C and allowed it to cook for another 20 minutes.) NB: Let the rack rest for 5–6 minutes before slicing.
8. To make the celery root purée, in a pot combine the celery root, water, non-dairy creamer, salt and pepper and bring to a simmer.
9. Cook for about 45 minutes, until the celery root is tender.
10. Strain through a colander and reserve the cooking liquid to add back to the purée if the consistency needs to be adjusted.
11. Put the celery root in a food processor, add the margarine and purée until smooth. If the consistency is too thick, you can add some of the cooking liquid back into the purée.
12. Serve the rack of lamb on a bed of celery purée and spoon the caramelised onions over the meat.
13. Finally decorate with a sprig or two of fried rosemary.

SERVES 6

CARNE DE ALHO PICANTE aka CUBED SPICY GARLIC BEEF aka TRINCHADO

This is a wonderful Sukkot meal in that you can make it in bulk, keep it in the fridge for up to three days and know that it gets better with age.

⅓ cup cake flour or cornflour

1 Tbsp Bisto gravy powder

1.5 kg side bolo steak, cubed

little oil for frying

2 onions, peeled and chopped

6–8 cloves garlic, crushed

2 hot chillies, finely shredded, or 1 Tbsp Nando's Hot Peri-Peri Sauce or homemade chilli sauce
   (see page 25)

½ cup red wine (you can use water instead – but I wouldn't!)

2 Tbsp tomato paste

1 tsp sugar

2 bay leaves

2 Tbsp soy sauce

1 cup beef broth or 1 beef stock cube dissolved in 1 cup water

1. Sprinkle the flour or cornflour and gravy powder over the beef cubes, ensuring that all the pieces are well coated.
2. Heat a little oil in a medium-sized saucepan and fry the beef cubes in small batches, ensuring that they brown on all sides. Too much meat cooked at once tends to boil and not brown. You may need to add a drop of oil between frying each batch.
3. Once cooked, remove the beef from the saucepan and set aside. Repeat until all the meat is cooked. I like to use a saucepan rather than a frying pan, as the surface area of a frying pan is too large, causing the sauce to evaporate too quickly and leaving the beef a little dried out.
4. When all the meat is cooked, add a little more oil to the same saucepan and fry the onions until golden brown.
5. Add the garlic and chillies or peri-peri/chilli sauce and stir. Continue to cook for about 2 minutes.
6. Add the wine and bring to the boil, stirring continuously. Allow the alcohol to evaporate for 2–3 minutes.
7. Return the meat to the pan.
8. Add the tomato paste, sugar, bay leaves, soy sauce and beef broth or stock and continue stirring.
9. Bring to the boil, reduce the heat and simmer with the lid on for about 40 minutes.
10. Remove the pan from the heat and set aside for a while to absorb all the lovely flavours. This is important.
11. Reheat when ready to serve.
12. Serve on a bed of rice with a hunk of bread for dunking.

SERVES 6

mafia meatballs IN HOMEMADE ITALIAN TOMATO SAUCE

My family loves Italian food – we eat an Italian meal once a week. I even chose my husband because he looks Italian! This tomato sauce can be used as a base for many different dishes so it may be worth your while to double up and freeze in individual Ziploc™ bags.

HOMEMADE TOMATO SAUCE

3 Tbsp olive oil
1 large onion, peeled and chopped
4 cloves garlic, crushed
1 fresh hot chilli (optional)
8–10 ripe red jam tomatoes or 2 x 410 g
cans chopped peeled tomatoes
1 Tbsp brown sugar
¾ cup boiling water
1 x 65 g can tomato paste
⅓ cup red wine (optional)
35 g fresh basil leaves, chopped (reserve
a little to sprinkle on top of the pasta)
salt and freshly ground black pepper
to taste

MEATBALLS

1 kg beef mince
1 onion, peeled and chopped
1 Tbsp chopped fresh parsley or 1 tsp dried
½ cup cornflake crumbs
½ cup water
salt and freshly ground black pepper
to taste

little oil for frying meatballs
500 g spaghetti

1. First make the tomato sauce. Heat the oil in a frying pan and fry the onions until limp. Add the garlic and chilli (if using) and continue to fry for a further 1–2 minutes.
2. If you are using fresh tomatoes, bring a medium-sized saucepan of hot water to the boil. Dip the fresh tomatoes briefly into the water to loosen the skins. Drain and peel, then cut in half horizontally and gently scoop out the seeds.
3. Add the tomatoes, sugar, water, tomato paste, wine (if using) and basil to the pan.
4. Bring to the boil, then reduce the heat and simmer for 10–15 minutes until the sauce reduces a little.
5. Remove the sauce from the heat and blend with a hand blender or in a food processor until smooth.
6. Season with salt and pepper.
7. To make the meatballs, mix all the ingredients in a bowl until well combined.
8. Using your hands, roll the mixture into small balls.
9. Fry the meatballs in a little oil until golden brown. Set aside. (If you are short on time, roll the balls slightly larger than a pea and just add them to the sauce and cook them through on a low heat for 10–15 minutes. After 10 minutes, take one out to check if it has cooked through. If not, leave it a little longer.)
10. Cook the pasta as per the packet instructions.
11. Reheat the meatballs in the homemade tomato sauce.
12. Pour over the spaghetti, toss and sprinkle with the reserved chopped basil.

SERVES 4–6

BILTONG SOUFFLÉ on a pool of mustard sauce

As soon as a person hears the word 'soufflé' they immediately think 'Oy vey'. Have no fear with this recipe, because if it does sink in a little when you remove it from the oven you can just place a couple of slices of shredded biltong in the 'pothole'! It's as easy as that!

MUSTARD SAUCE	BILTONG SOUFFLÉ
1 Tbsp non-dairy margarine	little olive oil or non-dairy margarine
1 Tbsp mustard seeds	for greasing
1 tsp mustard powder	little cake flour or some cornflake crumbs
2 tsp cornflour	for coating
pinch of salt	2 Tbsp non-dairy margarine
½ tsp freshly ground black pepper	2 heaped Tbsp cake flour
1 cup non-dairy creamer	1 cup soy milk
½ cup water	8 eggs, separated
¼ cup mayonnaise	250 g very finely shredded biltong (you may
	need to pulse it a couple of times in a food
	processor or chop it further – but keep a
	couple of the larger pieces for decorating)

1. To make the mustard sauce, melt the margarine over a medium to high heat. Remove from the heat and add the mustard seeds, mustard powder, cornflour, salt and pepper. Combine well. Still off the heat, add the non-dairy creamer and water, then return to the heat and heat through until just simmering, whisking all the time.
2. Once it starts to thicken, remove from the heat, cover and allow to stand at room temperature for about 30 minutes to absorb all the mustard flavours. Add the mayonnaise and refrigerate or leave at room temperature if you are going to use it within the next hour. Reheat just before serving.
3. Preheat the oven to 200 °C. Grease 8 ramekins with a little olive oil or non-dairy margarine.
4. Sprinkle the insides of the greased ramekins with a little flour or some cornflake crumbs. Roll the ramekins around so that the sides are evenly coated and then shake out the excess.
5. Melt the margarine in a large saucepan over a medium heat. Remove from the heat and add the flour. Mix well until it all comes together in a ball. Add the soy milk and whisk until there are no lumps to be seen.
6. Return to the heat, whisking all the while, until it starts to boil and thicken. Remove from the heat and cool slightly. Then whisk in 1 egg yolk at a time. Once you have incorporated all of the yolks, add the biltong shavings.
7. Beat the egg whites in a separate bowl until firm. Add one-third of the whites to the biltong mixture and fold in gently. Once fully incorporated, add the remaining egg whites, folding in gently until well incorporated.
8. Divide the mixture between the ramekins. Place the ramekins in a large roasting dish half-filled with boiling water and bake for 20–25 minutes.
9. Remove from the oven and allow to cool. Gently remove the soufflés from the ramekins.
10. Place dollops of the hot mustard sauce onto individual serving plates and position the soufflés on top of the sauce.
11. On Shabbat, I serve mine at room temperature, baking them as close to Shabbat as possible.
12. Decorate with extra biltong pieces, loosely scattered around the plate.

SERVES 8

GLAZED BRISKET SLAB with red cabbage relish

At least one night in the sukkah, I do a deli theme: usually during Chol Hamoed where a deli 'vibe' goes down well. To start with, you can serve sausage wraps (see page 193), followed by a variety of different brisket ideas. This is one option.

1½ kg ready-cooked smoked brisket (when ordering this, ask your butcher to leave it as a whole piece)

GLAZE
⅓ cup honey
⅓ cup brown sugar
⅓ cup tomato sauce
1 Tbsp red wine vinegar

1. Preheat the oven to 160 °C.
2. Wash the brisket under cold running water to remove any excess salt and pat dry with a paper towel.
3. Cut two large pieces of foil and position them on a flat surface, one running lengthways and the other on top of it running widthwise. Place the brisket in the centre and gently lift it all into a roasting pan.
4. In a bowl, mix all the glaze ingredients until well blended and pour over the brisket.
5. Draw the sides of the foil up to the centre and 'balloon' the foil around the meat so that there's a pocket of air between the meat and the foil.
6. Bake for about 1½ hours, by which time you should have a soft tender brisket coated in a lovely sticky glaze.
7. Slice and serve on fresh rye bread with the red cabbage relish below.

SERVES 8–10

RED CABBAGE relish

1 red cabbage, finely shredded
1 large carrot, peeled and finely shredded
1 large red onion, peeled and thinly sliced
2 large red peppers, deseeded and finely shredded

SALAD DRESSING
¾ cup red wine vinegar
1 cup olive oil

¼ cup fresh lime juice
¼ cup finely chopped coriander
¼ cup brown sugar
2 tsp finely grated orange zest
pinch of ground allspice
1 Tbsp cumin seeds or ½ tsp ground cumin
1 bay leaf
1–1½ tsp salt
1 tsp ground black pepper

1. Blanch the cabbage in a large saucepan of boiling salted water. You literally drop all the cabbage into the boiling water, ensure it's immersed and then remove it once it's all been dunked!
2. Drain well in a colander and allow to cool.
3. Transfer to a large bowl and toss with the carrot, onion and paprika peppers. Set aside.
4. To make the dressing, whisk all the ingredients together in a bowl or shake up in a jar.
5. Once the sugar has dissolved, let it stand for 20–30 minutes, remove the bay leaf and pour over the red cabbage relish. Serve immediately.

bunny's CHOW

Now, 'lettuce' see!

3 Tbsp oil	1 tsp ground turmeric
2 medium onions, peeled and chopped	1 tsp coarsely ground black pepper
35 g fresh coriander, chopped	2 x 410 g cans chopped peeled tomatoes
1 tsp crushed garlic	1 tsp sugar
1 Tbsp finely grated fresh ginger	4 Tbsp oil
1 fresh hot chilli, deseeded and chopped	1 kg beef mince
1 tsp ground cumin	2 heads lettuce, coarsely shredded
	salt to taste

1. Heat the oil in a large frying pan and brown the onions.
2. Add the coriander, garlic, ginger and chilli and fry for a further 2 minutes.
3. Add the cumin, turmeric and black pepper and give a good stir.
4. Add the tomatoes and sugar and bring to the boil.
5. Once boiling, remove from the heat, cover with a lid and set aside.
6. Meanwhile, add the 4 Tbsp oil to another saucepan and fry the mince until golden brown. Keep breaking up the mince with a fork while stirring otherwise it will go lumpy. The secret to the hearty taste of this dish lies in the colour of the mince. You want to get it a dark golden colour. The bottom of the pan should also turn dark brown. However, you don't want it to burn, so keep an eye on it and keep mixing.
7. Add the tomato mixture to the meat, give it a good stir and bring to the boil. Scrape all the brown bits off the bottom of the pan.
8. Add the lettuce and continue to cook until the lettuce goes limp.
9. Season with salt and stir well.
10. Reduce the heat and simmer for about 20 minutes, with the lid on.
11. Turn off the heat and leave the pan on the stove for about 30 minutes, so that the mince can absorb the flavours.
12. Reheat when ready to serve.
13. Serve on a bed of rice or in a scooped-out bread bun.

SERVES 5–6

tropical dream ICE CREAM

The flavours in this ice cream will transport you from the palm leaves of your sukkah to the palm trees of a tropical island. How often does it happen that you have two or three bananas left on a bunch that nobody eats? Instead of throwing them away, peel them, cut them into 2 cm chunks and freeze them. Then, once you've saved enough, defrost them and make this recipe. Or you can just buy a bunch of really ripe bananas and make it immediately.

½ cup sugar	1 tsp vanilla essence
2 Tbsp non-dairy margarine	½ tsp ground cinnamon
1 small pineapple, chopped	pinch of salt
6–8 bananas, peeled and cubed	2 cups non-dairy creamer, whipped
1 x 400 ml can coconut milk	with ⅓ cup icing sugar

1. In a medium to large saucepan, melt the sugar in the margarine over a medium heat.
2. Once the sugar has melted, add the pineapple and fry for 6–8 minutes until soft.
3. Add the bananas and continue to fry until soft.
4. Add the coconut milk, vanilla, cinnamon and salt and continue to stir as the milk warms through.
5. Just before it starts to boil, remove from the heat.
6. Blend the mixture until smooth, either with a hand blender or in a food processor.
7. Place in a freezerproof dish (big enough for the contents to double in size once you add the whipped creamer later) and freeze.
8. After 4–5 hours, remove from the freezer, scrape the frozen edges around the sides into the middle of the ice cream, mix well and then beat in the whipped creamer with an electric beater until well combined. Don't beat in the creamer until the ice cream has started to freeze (about two-thirds frozen) as it may separate.
9. Return to the freezer and freeze overnight.
10. Remove from the freezer 15–20 minutes before serving.
11. Serve with crispy coconut triangles (see below).

CRISPY COCONUT TRIANGLES

1 wrap/laffa/tortilla
1 Tbsp apricot jam
sprinkling of sugar and cinnamon
1 Tbsp desiccated coconut

1. Preheat the oven to 160 °C.
2. Place a sheet of baking paper on a baking tray (this is important, otherwise the wrap will stick to the tray).
3. Place the wrap/laffa/tortilla on the lined tray and spread the apricot jam over it.
4. Sprinkle with the sugar and cinnamon, and the coconut. Cut into 8–12 triangles.
5. Bake for about 15 minutes until golden brown and the jam starts to bubble a little.
6. Remove from the oven and allow to cool. They will crisp up.

SERVES 8–10

GRILLED NECTARINES and ginger cream

Because of their water content, nectarines cook quickly, which helps when you're in a hurry!

6 nectarines
12 Tbsp demerara sugar mixed with ½ tsp ground cinnamon
juice of 1 orange

1. Put on the oven grill and ensure that the oven rack is on the middle shelf.
2. Cut the nectarines in half from the top down, twist and carefully remove their pips with a teaspoon or knife.
3. Place the nectarines in an ovenproof dish cut side up.
4. Place 1 Tbsp of the cinnamon sugar in each nectarine half.
5. Sprinkle the orange juice over the fruit.
6. Grill until golden brown.
7. Serve warm, at room temperature or cold with a spoonful of ginger cream (see below) or ice cream.

GINGER CREAM

1 cup non-dairy creamer
4 pieces preserved ginger in syrup, chopped small

1. Beat the non-dairy creamer and gently fold in the ginger.
2. If ginger is not your thing, you can substitute it with the pulp of 1–2 granadillas.

SERVES 6–8

CHANUKKAH

CHANUKKAH

After defeating the Syrian-Greek army, the Maccabees entered Jerusalem and found the Holy Temple in a shambles. When it came to lighting the menorah, which burned 24/7, there was only enough oil for one day, but miraculously it burnt for eight, giving the Maccabees time to make more oil. It is, therefore, customary to eat foods fried in oil on Chanukkah to symbolise this miracle.

A couple of years back we were in America over Chanukkah and it was something I'll never forget or, rather, Chanukkah is something America won't let you forget!

The department stores glistened with blue and silver Chanukkah decorations and piped Chanukkah songs in the background. Giant menorahs glowed in shop windows. TV stations featured the most wonderful cookery programmes demonstrating every variation of latke imaginable.

In this section, I have included different recipe ideas for each of the eight nights. A twist here and there on tradition, but definitely worth frying!

Who says the festival of lights has to have anything to do with 'lite'?

beachroot SOUP

Chanukkah usually falls over the summer holidays in South Africa and the coast is where most of us like to go. What could be better than an ice-cold glass of beetroot soup on a boiling hot beachy day? I could think of nothing better, but then I could think of nothing worse than having to boil, peel and grate beetroot on my holiday. So here's the delicious solution to all your problems.

1 vegetable stock cube	½ cup non-dairy creamer (I use 1 x 125 ml
1 cup boiling water	sachet Orley Whip™ Cook 'n Crème)
1 x 780 g bottle grated beetroot	1 cucumber, finely chopped
1½ cups cold water	handful of fresh coriander, finely chopped
2 Tbsp sugar	(optional)

1. Dissolve the vegetable stock cube in the boiling water and set aside to cool.
2. Place the beetroot, with its juice, in a blender or food processor with the cooled vegetable stock, water and sugar. Blend until smooth.
3. Refrigerate until really cold. I usually make it in the morning to have in the early evening.
4. Before serving, stir and taste again as it may need a little more sweetness; that depends on you.
5. Pour into individual glasses and, just before serving, drizzle each with a little non-dairy creamer and sprinkle with the cucumber and coriander.

SERVES 6–8

YE OLDE ENGLISH chish and fips

'Nobody,' and my husband says that quite confidently, 'makes deep-fried battered fish like your mother!'

To ensure that the fish is encased in a batter that puffs out into a balloon of crisp golden-brown perfection, she does have some very strict rules: The batter has to be silky smooth, the oil very hot and it has to be eaten the moment it comes out of the frying pan.

BATTER
2 cups self-raising flour
½ cup cornflour
1 tsp salt
1 x 340 ml can beer (beer can be substituted with water)

1 kg skinned and filleted hake, cut into fingers
oil for frying

1. Whisk the batter ingredients together until smooth. The batter should have the consistency of pourable custard. If it needs more liquid, add a little water, one tablespoon at a time.
2. Dip the fish fingers into the batter.
3. Deep-fry in hot oil until golden brown.
4. Drain and serve immediately with hot chips – immediately is the secret to crispy batter!

TIP: If there is any batter left over, take an onion, cut it into quarters and separate the leaves. Place the onion leaves in the batter, mix to ensure they are well coated, and deep-fry. Serve with Za'atar Aioli (see page 189).

SERVES 4–5

summertime **STEAK SALAD**

When I see the word 'summertime', I can almost hear this song playing in the background: 'Summertime, and the living is easy … seaside holidays make it all worthwhile. Comes the summer and we all need to rush there, to the blue of the sea and the sky …' Before I start getting all caught up in this song, I just wanted to add that this is also a wonderful salad for Shabbat. The steak can be prepared the day before, refrigerated and brought to room temperature the next day.

MARINADE
½ cup olive oil
½ cup soy sauce
1 tsp peanut butter
juice of 1 lime (about 2 Tbsp)
¼ cup orange juice
2 Tbsp finely grated fresh ginger
1 tsp crushed fresh garlic
1 small fresh hot chilli or 1 Tbsp hot chilli sauce (see page 25)
2 heaped Tbsp brown treacle sugar
35 g coriander, finely chopped

2 side bolos (ask the butcher to cut them in half along the length of the white sinew and to remove
   the sinew so that you are left with 2 large long steaks). As this recipe calls for 2 side bolos, you will
   have 4 steaks of about 20 cm long and 1 cm thick.
freshly ground black pepper
sesame seeds and pine nut kernels to serve

1. Combine the marinade ingredients in a mixing bowl. If you don't feel like chopping and grating, you can place all the marinade ingredients in a food processor and pulse it a few times, or you could use a hand blender.
2. Pour over the steaks and allow to marinate for a day or two.
3. When ready to cook, remove the steaks from the marinade. Don't throw away the marinade as you will need to heat it up later. Heating it up is very important from a health point of view, because you cannot pour marinade that has been tenderising raw meat onto cooked meat.
4. Either fry or braai the steaks whole. They only need 4–5 minutes per side, as you want them to be pink inside.
5. Once cooked to your specifications, remove the steaks from the heat and place in a dish. Cover and allow them to stand for about 15 minutes.
6. After 15 minutes you will see that they have given off their own juices. This is like gold! Add these juices to the marinade and bring to the boil in a saucepan on the stove.
7. Once boiling, reduce the heat and simmer for 3–4 minutes.
8. Pour the marinade over the cooked steaks, grind some black pepper over them and slice (across the grain) into thin slivers.
9. Serve at room temperature on a bed of mixed lettuce leaves and sprinkle with sesame seeds and pine nut kernels.

SERVES 10–12

justa very loud PASTA SALAD

It was my son Ryan's birthday and he had a few friends over for Shabbat supper. They all got stuck into one particular salad at the same time and from that end of the table it sounded like rocks being crushed by a steamroller. I've often been asked 'What's in this salad?', but I've never been asked 'What's making this a very loud salad?' So this one's for you, Justin; just don't eat it in a library!

250 g gnocchi pasta (cooked as per packet instructions)
oil for frying
5–6 spring onions, chopped into 1 cm pieces
250 g baby tomatoes
chopped basil or flat-leaf parsley for decoration

DRESSING
3 Tbsp pesto sauce (Mooz and Norries are pareve)
⅓ cup Italian salad dressing
⅓ cup pasta sauce (I use Gefen or All Joy)
⅓ cup mayonnaise

1. Once the gnocchi has boiled, wash it in cold water and drain well.
2. Heat the oil in a deep frying pan and fry the pasta in small batches until golden brown and crispy. Remove and drain on paper towels or brown paper.
3. The fried pasta can be made up to three days in advance and stored at room temperature in an airtight container. It shouldn't go soft, but if it does, put it into a preheated oven at 180 °C for 10–12 minutes to crisp up. Then you can make an even louder crunch!
4. When ready to assemble, place the pasta into a serving bowl, sprinkle with the spring onions and add the tomatoes.
5. To make the dressing, combine the ingredients.
6. Just before serving, pour the dressing over the pasta, toss and serve immediately, decorated with the chopped basil or flat-leaf parsley.

SERVES 10–12

LE CHAIM cucumbers

Most men love nothing better than a whisky, a piece of krakelwurst and a couple of Le Chaim cucumbers to unwind quietly at the end of the day. Oops, I nearly forgot one thing: and not to be asked 'What are you thinking?'

3 kg Israeli cucumbers
2 litres water
2½ cups vinegar
18 cloves garlic, peeled
5 bay leaves
½ cup sugar
½ cup coarse salt

1. Wash and slice the cucumbers into 1 cm-thick slices. This may seem thicker than usual, but it works well for this.
2. Place all the ingredients, except the cucumbers, in a large saucepan and simmer until the sugar dissolves. Set aside and allow to cool.
3. Place the cucumber slices in glass jars and cover with the pickling solution.

SERVES A LOT (DON'T WORRY, YOU'LL HAVE ENOUGH!)

BEST CORN SALAD under the sun

Here is a salad that's easy to make on holiday. So simple, so tasty and yet it must be one of my most frequently requested recipes. It keeps for about three or four days in the fridge.

1 kg frozen corn kernels, defrosted
1 large or 2 medium onions, peeled and finely chopped
1½ cups mayonnaise
salt and pepper to taste

1. Place the corn, onions, mayonnaise, salt and pepper in a salad bowl and mix until well combined.

SERVES 10

PASTRAMI LATKES with sweet-chilli mayo

Don't dreidel *your* kop *and get into a spin looking for recipes, because here is a latke recipe definitely worth frying!*

3 large potatoes
1 large onion, peeled
1 egg
½ cup cornflour
1 tsp baking powder
salt and pepper to taste
250 g pastrami, shredded
oil for frying

1. Peel the potatoes and immediately immerse them in cold water to prevent them from turning brown.
2. Grate the onion and place in a bowl large enough to hold the potatoes as well.
3. Remove the potatoes from the water and grate them on the large hole side of the grater. Strain the excess water off the grated potatoes, then add to the onion and mix well.
4. Lightly beat the egg with a fork and add to the grated vegetables.
5. Add the cornflour, baking powder, salt and pepper and mix well.
6. Finally, add the shredded pastrami and mix until well combined.
7. Pour oil into a frying pan, to a quarter way up the sides of the pan, and heat on the stove.
8. Spoon heaped tablespoons of the mixture into the hot oil, flatten them slightly to ensure even cooking and fry until golden brown.
9. Serve with a bowl of sweet-chilli mayo, made by mixing ½ cup sweet chilli sauce with ½ cup mayonnaise.
10. Alternatively, make up a mustard-mayo-pickle sauce by mixing ½ cup chopped pickled cucumber with ½ cup mayonnaise and 2 tsp ready-made Dijon mustard.

SERVES 10

zucchini and mushroom LATKES WITH ZA'ATAR AIOLI

This gluten-free recipe contains all the good-guy ingredients! Baby marrow or zucchini is packed with vitamin C, and mushrooms, although we know don't leave 'mush room' for anything else, are a wonderful source of potassium. The olive oil that the latkes are fried in keeps our skin glowing and the Za'atar spice helps with digestion. No excuses, here's to our health over Chanukkah – Lechaim!

600 g baby marrow/zucchini, grated
2 tsp salt
250 g mushrooms, sliced
1 large onion, peeled and grated
½–¾ cup cornflake crumbs
2 eggs, lightly beaten
1 tsp curry powder
oil for frying

1. Place the grated marrow in a bowl, add the salt, toss and evenly distribute. Allow to stand for about 20 minutes.
2. After 20 minutes, transfer to a colander and press out the excess water.
3. Return to the bowl and add the mushrooms, onion, cornflake crumbs, eggs and curry powder. If you find the mixture too loose, add more cornflake crumbs. Mix well.
4. Preheat the oven to 160 °C.
5. Heat the oil, which should be about 1 cm deep, in the frying pan. Place one heaped tablespoon of the mixture into the hot oil and flatten with the back of a spoon. Fry until golden brown (3–4 minutes per side), remove and drain on absorbent paper towels or brown paper, then transfer to the oven to keep warm while you fry the rest.
6. This mixture can also be prepared the day before and kept in the fridge until ready to fry.
7. Serve with Za'atar Aioli (see below). This is a Middle Eastern spice available at most kosher supermarkets and fine-food stores. It's the herbs and spices you see in Israel on top of pitas, flatbreads, hummus and tahini.

ZA'ATAR AIOLI
2 large cloves garlic, peeled
1 cup mayonnaise
1 Tbsp fresh lemon juice
¼ cup olive oil
2 Tbsp Za'atar spice (if you are unable to get this spice, then combine 1 tsp paprika, 1 tsp dried thyme, 1 tsp ground cumin and 1 Tbsp ground sesame seeds)
salt and pepper to taste

1. Place the garlic, mayonnaise and lemon juice in a food processor.
2. Switch it on and, with the machine running, add the oil in a thin stream, blending until smooth.
3. Transfer to a small bowl and whisk in the Za'atar spice. Season with salt and pepper and allow to stand for at least 30 minutes to allow the flavours to develop. This can be made the day before.

MAKES 12–15 LATKES

cheeseless PIZZA

A pizza without cheese sounds like pasta without sauce! But once you've tried this version, you may never go back to cheese again! It's all in the fresh, herbed tomato sauce with added mince, which creates a delicious base on which to build your own towering pizza. If you don't fancy making your own dough, you can use tortillas, pitas or ready-made pareve pizza bases instead.

PIZZA DOUGH	HEARTY MINCED BEEF
3 cups all-purpose flour	tomato sauce (see page 165)
1 x 10 g pkt instant yeast	1 large onion, peeled and finely chopped
1 cup warm water	little oil for frying
⅓ cup oil	½ cup water
1 tsp salt	500 g beef mince
2 tsp sugar	salt and pepper to taste

1. Place all the pizza dough ingredients in a bowl and mix to form a dough. You may need to add a little more water.
2. Place the dough in a bowl, cover with cling film and set aside to rise for 45 minutes.
3. Start making the tomato sauce for the mince while you wait. Make up a batch using the recipe on page 165 (Mafia Meatballs). You will need 2–2½ cups of the tomato sauce to mix with the mince.
4. To make the mince, fry the onion in a little oil until golden brown.
5. Add the water and scrape all the dark brown bits off the bottom of the pan.
6. Add the mince and continue to cook, stirring continuously, until the mince has cooked through and is a little brown on the edges.
7. Remove from the heat and add the tomato sauce. Mix until well combined and season with salt and pepper.
8. After 45 minutes, punch down the dough and divide it into 8 equal portions. Roll into balls, place on a lightly floured baking tray and cover with cling film. Allow to rise for a further 10 minutes.
9. Preheat the oven to 240 °C.
10. Roll out the balls of dough on a well-floured surface to your desired size (the bigger you roll them, the thinner the crust will be) and carefully place on a lightly oiled and floured baking tray.
11. Smear 5–6 Tbsp of the mince onto each pizza base. You can put more, depending on the size of the pizza, but don't take it all the way to the edge; leave about 1 cm free all the way around.
12. Add a layer of very thinly sliced salami or krakelwurst (I prefer the latter as it has a smaller diameter). You could also use thinly sliced Russian sausage.
13. Now you can start having fun and adding whatever other toppings you desire.
14. When your masterpieces are complete, bake in the oven for 6–8 minutes. Ovens vary in temperature, so keep an eye on your pizzas. I would hate for you to burn them!

INGREDIENT IDEAS FOR BUILDING YOUR PIZZA:
asparagus; artichokes; avocados; caramelised onions; chillies; garlic; mushrooms; olives; red, green and yellow peppers; thinly sliced roasted vegetables – baby marrow, aubergine, butternut and onion

MAKES 8 PIZZAS

sausage **WRAPS**

Get ready to roll, because these are going to be your children's and your own NBCs (new best cravings)!

1 x 104 g pkt Cadbury Original Smash or homemade mashed potato (from 3 large potatoes)
500 g frozen puff pastry
1 kg (18–20) Vienna sausages
1 egg yolk lightly beaten with 2 Tbsp cold water
¼ cup sesame seeds

1. Make the Smash as per the packet instructions or make up your own mashed potatoes. The mashed potato needs to be quite firm.
2. Unroll the pastry and roll it out quite thinly, to double its original size (length and breadth).
3. Cut the pastry into squares big enough for a sausage to fit on the diagonal. Don't worry too much if the sausage sticks out of the sides of the pastry.
4. Turn each pastry square so that it looks like a diamond, with a point facing you.
5. Place 2 Tbsp of the Smash or mashed potatoes in the middle of each diamond and spread it out a little (not over the entire piece of pastry).
6. Place a sausage horizontally in the centre and wrap the pastry around it, starting with the bottom-most point, gently rolling it up like a rugelach. Rolling it too tightly will cause the mash to ooze out.
7. Paint each wrap with the egg wash and sprinkle with the sesame seeds.
8. These can be frozen at this point (before baking). Freeze them individually first then, once completely frozen, place in Ziploc™ bags. If you don't freeze them individually first, they'll stick together.
9. When ready to bake, preheat the oven to 180 °C. Place the sausage wraps on a baking tray and bake until golden brown for 15–20 minutes.

TIP: For a cocktail-party snack, use cocktail Viennas to make smaller, bite-size wraps.

SERVES 18–20 (G-D HELP ANYBODY IF THEY WANT SECONDS!)

ITALIAN SALAMI tart

This is a firm favourite when you quickly need to whip up something as a starter to nosh on while you're waiting for the steaks to come off the braai!

1 x 400 g pkt puff pastry
3 Tbsp pesto sauce
1 tsp crushed fresh garlic
1 Tbsp tomato paste
1 tsp brown sugar
4–5 red Rosa tomatoes, thinly sliced
1 large red onion, peeled and very thinly sliced
handful of fresh basil leaves, roughly chopped
250 g salami, very thinly sliced
salt and freshly ground black pepper to taste

1. Preheat the oven to 180 °C.
2. Roll out the pastry to fit a flat baking tray. As pastry shrinks when baked, roll it slightly larger than the tray.
3. Prick the pastry carefully with a fork here and there.
4. Bake it in the oven for 15 minutes, then remove and allow to cool.
5. Increase the oven temperature to 190 °C.
6. Combine the pesto, garlic, tomato paste and sugar and spread over the pastry base.
7. Place the tomato slices in rows on top of the pesto, followed by the onion, basil and, finally, the salami. Season with salt and pepper.
8. Return to the oven and bake for 20–25 minutes until golden brown. Serve immediately.

SERVES 8–10

CHICKEN WITH PINE NUTS and basil-scented tomatoes

If I could give you one tip with this recipe, it would be to get everything ready in advance, just as they do on the cooking programmes. The success of this dish lies in the speed at which it's cooked and the speed at which you can get everybody to the table. If your family's like mine, the latter may be more difficult!

5 Tbsp olive oil	35 g basil leaves
2 Tbsp lemon juice	1 Tbsp crushed or finely chopped fresh
6 thick chicken schnitzels, each cut	rosemary needles
into 3	1 Tbsp brown sugar
freshly ground black pepper to taste	½ cup white wine or chicken stock
1 red onion, peeled and sliced	3 Tbsp pine nuts
3 cloves garlic, crushed	250 g baby tomatoes

1. Heat 3 Tbsp of the oil in a large frying pan over a medium to high heat.
2. Sprinkle the lemon juice over the chicken, mix well and then season with the black pepper.
3. Fry the chicken for 2–3 minutes per side until browned.
4. Lower the heat and allow the chicken to cook through. You can cook it in batches.
5. As you fry them, transfer the chicken pieces to a large dish and cover with foil to keep warm.
6. To the same pan in which you fried the chicken, add 1 Tbsp oil and fry the onions until soft. Add the garlic, basil and rosemary and cook for about 3 minutes.
7. Add the sugar, wine or chicken stock and bring to the boil. Scrape all the brown bits off the bottom of the pan before pouring the whole lot over the chicken. Re-cover with foil to retain the heat.
8. Add a drop more oil to the pan, add the pine nuts and cook for 1–2 minutes until they start to turn brown.
9. Finally, add the tomatoes and cook for a further 2–3 minutes. You don't want the tomatoes to be too soft; that's why we add them at the end.
10. Return the chicken and juices to the pan just to heat through, and serve immediately on a bed of rice.

SERVES 5–6

garlic CHICKEN ROLLOVERS

With a little substitution here and there, these are great during Pesach as well. When you feel like a little 'something' to fill the gap that a bagel would normally fill, try these.

8 chicken schnitzels
4 Tbsp non-dairy margarine
2 Tbsp cornflake crumbs (during Pesach, use matzo meal instead)
2 tsp crushed fresh garlic
2 tsp dried parsley
½ cup cake flour (during Pesach, leave this out – matzo sticks well enough to the egg)
2 eggs, beaten
2 cups cornflake crumbs (during Pesach, use matzo meal instead)
little oil for frying

1. Place each chicken schnitzel between two sheets of cling film.
2. Flatten them by rolling with a heavy rolling pin, giving them a light bashing every now and then, which helps to get them flatter and thinner (about 3 mm thin).
3. Combine the margarine, 2 Tbsp cornflake crumbs, garlic and parsley in a bowl and mix to form a paste.
4. Spread about a tablespoon of the paste onto the side of each chicken schnitzel facing you.
5. Turn the long sides of the chicken schnitzels in (about 2 cm) and roll them up as you would a Swiss roll. Secure each with a toothpick.
6. Dip the chicken rolls first into the flour, then into the beaten egg and finally into the 2 cups cornflake crumbs.
7. At this point you can freeze the chicken rollovers individually on a tray. Once frozen, place them in a Ziploc™ bag and store in the freezer.
8. To cook, preheat the oven to 180 °C.
9. Heat the oil in a frying pan and fry the chicken rollovers until golden brown on all sides. Use the toothpick to put them into the pan and then, when ready to turn over, lift the chicken with tongs and push the toothpick through so that you can brown the other side without the toothpick being in the way. They shouldn't be fried too long as they are still going to be baked in the oven.
10. Remove the rollovers from the pan and place on a baking tray.
11. Bake for 10–15 minutes. Remember that, although the chicken may be brown on the outside, it has been rolled and will take a little longer to cook all the way through.

SERVES 6–8 (DEPENDING ON HOW HUNGRY EVERYONE IS!)

CHICKEN drumstix

Another idea for the forever-hungry teens to nosh on after a hard rugby or soccer match are these drumstix. They are also great in school lunch boxes.

½ cup grape jam
1 cup tomato cocktail
1 Tbsp lemon juice
1 tsp salt
8 chicken drumsticks

1. Preheat the oven to 160 °C.
2. Combine the grape jam, tomato juice, lemon juice and salt, mix until smooth and pour over the chicken drumsticks. Ensure they are well coated.
3. Place the drumsticks and sauce in a small roasting pan so that they fit comfortably, cover with foil and roast for 1 hour. Remove the foil and roast, uncovered, for another hour.
4. If the roasting pan is too big the sauce will evaporate too quickly. The whole idea of these drumsticks is that they cook on a lower temperature for a longer period of time, which gives them a lovely toffee-ish glaze.

MAKES 8

delicious stuffing CRUMBED CHICKEN SCHNITZELS

That's stuffed things up! It's not inside; it's on top!

1 cup soy milk
2 Tbsp lemon juice
2 Tbsp mayonnaise
8 chicken schnitzels
1 x 100 g pkt Ina Paarman's™ Sage
and Onion Stuffing Mix

1 cup cornflake crumbs
½ tsp garlic powder
½ tsp ground paprika
½ tsp lemon pepper
oil for frying

1. Combine the soy milk, lemon juice and mayonnaise in a mixing bowl, pour over the chicken schnitzels and leave to marinate overnight.
2. In a separate bowl, combine the stuffing mix, cornflake crumbs, garlic powder, paprika and lemon pepper.
3. Remove the chicken schnitzels from the marinade and dip straight into the crumbed mixture.
4. Heat the oil in a frying pan and fry the schnitzels until golden brown.
5. Serve with Best Corn Salad Under the Sun (see page 184).

SERVES 6 (OR 8 NOT-SO HUNGRY, BUT YOU'LL WANT TO MAKE MORE FOR LUNCH THE NEXT DAY!)

come-rain-or-shine LASAGNE

Whether it's miserable and overcast or gloriously sunny, there comes a time when you're maxed-out on braais and a lasagne will go down well. Make up a few in medium-sized foil containers and freeze. You should be able to make up at least two medium-sized foil containers with this quantity. I promise you'll wish you'd made more!

little oil for frying
2 onions, peeled and chopped
1 tsp brown sugar
1 kg beef mince
2 cups Nussbaums chicken soup or 2 chicken stock cubes dissolved in 2 cups water
1 x 115 g can tomato paste
1 x 410 g can chopped peeled tomatoes
1 tsp crushed fresh garlic
35 g fresh basil, chopped
salt and pepper to taste
1 x 250 g box lasagne pasta (ensure that it is the no-need-to-boil-first variety)

WHITE SAUCE
4 heaped Tbsp cornflour
1 cup soy milk
2 cups cold chicken soup
1 cup non-dairy creamer (I use 1 x 250 ml box Orley Whip™ Cook 'n Crème)

1. Heat the oil in a frying pan and fry the onions until golden brown. Add the brown sugar and stir.
2. Add the mince and fry until cooked through.
3. Add 1 cup of the chicken soup or stock, the tomato paste, tomatoes, garlic, basil, salt and pepper and bring to the boil, stirring continuously.
4. Once bubbling, reduce the heat and simmer for about 10 minutes with the lid lying loosely on top. You want the sauce to be quite liquid as the pasta will absorb some of the moisture while cooking.
5. Meanwhile, make the white sauce by dissolving the cornflour in the soy milk. Place this, along with the chicken soup and non-dairy creamer, in a saucepan on the stove and bring to the boil, whisking all the while. Once it starts to thicken, reduce the heat, keep whisking for another minute and then remove from the heat. The sauce should have a smooth, pourable consistency. If too thick, add a little more soy milk.
6. Preheat the oven to 180 °C.
7. Place a layer of white sauce on the bottom of an ovenproof dish or foil container, followed by a layer of mince, then pasta. Continue to layer in that order ending with a layer of white sauce. Freeze it at this point, as baking it now and then reheating will make it dry.
8. Bake in the oven for 25–30 minutes until bubbling and golden brown on top.

SERVES 6

double-dipped BBQ BEEF FINGERS AND POTA'TOES'

Whatever you do, don't double dip a cooked beef finger into the communal BBQ sauce. Dipping it once, then taking a bite and re-dipping it is an absolute no-no! Etiquette forbids this! Rather take a spoonful of the communal BBQ sauce, place it on your plate and then you can triple dip if you'd like to. Just as you wouldn't double dip a finger, don't double dip your potaTOES.

2 Tbsp soy sauce

1 cup tomato sauce (ketchup)

⅓ cup packed brown sugar

⅓ cup red wine vinegar

1 Tbsp Worcestershire sauce

freshly ground black pepper and a dash
  of salt to taste

3 large London broil steaks

1. Combine the soy sauce, tomato sauce, sugar, vinegar, Worcestershire sauce, pepper and salt in a mixing bowl.
2. Place the steaks and 1 cup of the marinade in a Ziploc™ bag and leave to marinate overnight or for the whole day in the fridge. Store the remaining marinade in the fridge too.
3. Remove the steaks from the bag and discard the marinade. Braai or fry the meat to the way you like it done.
4. Bring the remaining marinade to the boil in a small saucepan. Reduce the heat and simmer for 10–15 minutes, stirring occasionally, while it reduces by a third. It should have a thickish, sauce-like consistency. Pour into a small serving bowl.
5. When done, cut the steaks against the grain into fingers and arrange on a serving dish, with the bowl of sauce in the middle for dipping. Don't forget the DD rule!
6. Serve with French fries, which are also delicious when dipped in the sauce.

SERVES 4–5

glazed STEAKHOUSE RIBS

3 racks smoked steakhouse beef ribs (about 7 ribs per rack)

GLAZE

1 cup apricot jam

½ cup packed dark sugar

¼ cup apple cider vinegar

½ cup tomato sauce

1. Cut each rib individually.
2. Combine all the glaze ingredients and paint on each rib.
3. Braai, barbecue or roast the ribs – as they are smoked already, they are cooked. All you need to do is heat them through and crisp them up.

SERVES 6–7 (3 RIBS PER PERSON, BUT IF IT WERE MY SONS AND THEIR FRIENDS, 1 RACK PER PERSON!)

TEXAN RODEO steaks

You don't get bigger or better than a Texan Rodeo. Well, that's what they tell me in Texas! And you don't want to mess with Texas! 'Rodeo' comes from the Spanish word 'rodear', which means to encircle or surround and that's exactly what this steak does. It encircles a bone from which it receives optimum flavour. Meat with a bone shouldn't be wet-aged in a vacuum bag for too long and, as it's difficult to dry-age meat in a domestic fridge, I have a little trick up my sleeve for you! Don't let your husbands or wives tell you it sounds like a fruit salad, just do it on the QT.

QUICK TENDERISING MARINADE
½ small pineapple (use the rest for a fruit salad)
1 small paw-paw, roughly chopped
½ cup oil
4 cm knob fresh ginger

4 Texan Rodeo steaks, cut 1 cm thick
little oil for rubbing
Robertson's Texan Sizzling Steak Seasoning or similar for sprinkling

1. Place all the marinade ingredients in a food processor and blend until smooth.
2. Pour a cup of the blended fruit marinade into the bottom of a large rectangular dish.
3. Place 2 steaks in the dish, side by side, and cover with another cup of the marinade.
4. Place the remaining steaks on top of the first two and cover with the rest of the marinade.
5. Cover the dish with cling film and refrigerate for 3–4 hours, no longer.
6. Remove the steaks from the dish, discard the marinade and wash the steaks well. Pat dry with paper towels.
7. Rub the steaks with a little oil and sprinkle with the Texan seasoning.
8. For best results, braai or barbecue the steaks. The next best option would be to fry them on a hot skillet.

SERVES 6–8

shotgun CHOCOLATE MOUSSE CAKE

Try this quick and easy dessert for something different.

2 x 1 litre tubs ready-made chocolate mousse from your favourite kosher deli or bakery
non-dairy chocolate or honeycomb for grating

1. Preheat the oven to 170 °C. Spread 1 tub of mousse into a 26 cm x 16 cm rectangular dish and bake for 20–25 minutes.
2. Remove from the oven and allow to cool. Spread the other tub of mousse over the baked mousse. Grate some non-dairy chocolate or honeycomb over the top and freeze.
3. Remove from the freezer about 20 minutes before serving, cut into squares and enjoy after your Texan steaks.

SERVES 6–8

Texan rodeo steaks

REDD'S CHANUKKAH APPLE FRITTERS with cinnamon sugar

Although Redd's has a minimal amount of alcohol, it does evaporate when cooked, like a beer batter, so these should be safe enough for children.

1 x 340 ml bottle Redd's Premium Cider (only the Premium is kosher)
1½–1¾ cups self-raising flour
2 Tbsp sugar
1 x 125 g pkt dried apple rings
oil for frying
1 Tbsp cinnamon mixed with 1 cup sugar

1. Pour the cider into a mixing bowl and add the flour and sugar. Whisk until smooth.
2. Place the dried apple rings in the batter and refrigerate until ready to fry.
3. When ready to cook, heat the oil in a frying pan over a medium to high heat.
4. Remove the apple rings from the batter, ensuring they are well coated and start frying the rings – not too many at once, otherwise they start to stick to one another and fry too quickly. Don't let the oil get too hot otherwise they will burn.
5. When golden brown, remove and drain on paper towels.
6. Sprinkle with the cinnamon sugar and serve.
7. If you find the batter isn't retaining its crispness, place the apple rings into a preheated oven at 170 °C for 5–6 minutes and they will crisp up.

YOU SHOULD GET ABOUT 20 APPLE RINGS PER 125 G PACKET

PURIM

PURIM

Esther, a beautiful Jewish girl, was chosen to be queen of Persia. Haman, advisor to King Ahasuerus at the time, planned to kill the Jews, but Esther foiled his plans. Haman was hanged from the gallows and Mordechai, Esther's uncle, became the king's advisor. Although this is the story in a nutshell, it is one of ultimate triumph against all odds, where hidden miracles unveiled themselves.

This one-day festival is traditionally celebrated by dressing up in fancy-dress costumes, listening to two readings of the Megilla (the story of Purim), giving money to the poor, giving *mishloach manot* (two different, ready-to-eat foods) to at least one friend and eating hamantaschen. Hamantaschen are triangular-shaped dough parcels, which some say are to remind us of Haman's pointy ears or his three-cornered hat. These delicious confectioneries contain a hidden filling (to remind us of the hidden miracles) of either poppy seeds, apples, jam or cream cheese.

Ask any adult if they remember what costume they wore on Purim and I guarantee you it will bring a smile to their face. Would you believe that each year we would dress at least one of our children as a walking 'Nussbaums advert' with stickers and dry wors hanging around their neck? What were we thinking? Probably the same thing my parents were thinking when they dressed us as doctors and painters – my grandfather was a doctor and my father had a paint factory!

We celebrate this colourful festival with absolute joy – not only is it Purim, but on this day in 2009 we were blessed with our first grandchildren, twin girls and our very own princesses, Clara Leah and Zahara Beila, and guess what? We'll continue to dress them up for Purim just as our grandparents and parents did with us, even if we don't know why! Tradition, tradition, tradition!

lentil and **CHICKPEA SOUP**

It is customary to eat grains and legumes on Purim, because Queen Esther had only these to eat, since she had no access to kosher foods in King Ahasuerus's palace.

1 cup dried lentils
1 cup dried chickpeas
½ cup small dried white beans
½ cup barley (use samp mealies as a gluten-free option)
oil for frying
2 onions, peeled and chopped
1 tsp crushed garlic
1 tsp ground cumin
6 large carrots, peeled and grated on large hole of grater
3 long celery sticks, chopped
handful of fresh parsley, chopped
4 litres water
2 Tbsp mushroom stock powder
2 Tbsp chicken stock powder
2 Tbsp krupnik soup powder (I use Telma®) (for a gluten-free option, leave this out and add more
   of the other stock)
salt and pepper to taste

1. Wash and check the lentils, chickpeas, white beans and barley in separate bowls. Cover with boiling water and allow to soak overnight. When ready to use, drain thoroughly, check and rinse again.
2. Heat the oil in a large pot and fry the onions until golden brown. Add the garlic and cumin and continue to fry for a further 2–3 minutes.
3. Add the carrots, celery and parsley and cook for a few minutes, stirring continuously.
4. Add the water and the drained lentils, chickpeas, white beans and barley.
5. Bring to the boil, reduce the heat and simmer for 2–3 hours. Check on the water every so often, as the legumes absorb a lot while cooking.
6. When the chickpeas are soft, add the stock/soup powders, give it a good stir and switch off the heat. Allow the soup to stand with the lid on for 1 hour while it thickens up.
7. Season with salt and pepper – this soup will need quite a bit of salt, because of the beans and barley.
8. Some people like to add potatoes to this kind of soup, which you can do, but I wouldn't add more than two or three medium potatoes (cubed) as the soup can become quite stodgy.

SERVES 8

purim **PASTA SALAD**

Although a day of fun, Purim can be quite busy. Try to get most of the food preparation done beforehand so that you can really enjoy the fun-filled day it is meant to be. For this salad, one can cut up all the vegetables the day before and store in little plastic bags in the fridge. The pasta can also be cooked the day before, drained and, once cool, placed in a bowl, covered with about two-thirds of the dressing and refrigerated. This prevents the pasta from sticking together. Then, just before serving, all you have to do is add the vegetables and a little more salad dressing.

> 250 g pasta (bow ties work well)
> handful of chopped carrots
> handful of chopped celery
> handful of cherry tomatoes
> handful of chopped cucumber
> handful of fresh corn
> handful of chopped peppers
> handful of chopped onion
> handful of chopped mushrooms
> handful of fresh peas
> handful of chopped spring onion
> handful of bean sprouts
> handful of anything else you'd like to add
> handful of love
> salt to bring out the flavour of all the lovely vegetables
> 1 cup of your favourite Italian salad dressing mixed with ½ cup mayonnaise and
>   2 heaped Tbsp poppy seeds
> handful of raw nuts

1. Cook the pasta according to the packet instructions.
2. Mix all the vegetables together, season with salt, add the cooked pasta and pour over the salad dressing.
3. Finally, sprinkle over the raw nuts just before serving.

SERVES 8

MEDITERRANEAN chicken parcels

On Purim, we symbolically eat foods that are 'hidden', reminding us of Hashem's concealed plans to save the Jewish people. In keeping with this tradition, I have included this recipe for wrapped Mediterranean chicken, which can be kept a secret until unwrapped at the table!

little oil for frying
1 whole chicken, cut into 8–10 pieces
2 heaped Tbsp hummus
1 x 410 g can Mediterranean-style ratatouille
10–12 pitted black olives
1 tsp crushed garlic
500 g baby potatoes
½ tsp salt
1 tsp freshly ground black pepper
1 tsp Greek-style dried spice blend

1. Heat the oil in a frying pan and brown the chicken.
2. Meanwhile, place a layer of heavy-duty foil in a roasting pan widthwise, extending beyond the width of the dish so that you have an overlap, then do the same lengthways.
3. Preheat the oven to 180 °C.
4. Place the chicken pieces in the centre of the foil, where the two pieces meet in the middle of the roasting pan.
5. Combine the hummus, ratatouille, olives and garlic in a bowl, mix well and pour over the chicken.
6. Wash the potatoes well and, leaving the skin on, cut them in half. Arrange them around the chicken.
7. Season the chicken and potatoes with the salt, pepper and Greek spice blend.
8. Pull up the sides of the foil and twist them in the middle to close.
9. Cook in the oven for 1 hour, then open the foil, reduce the heat to 170 °C and bake for a further 40–45 minutes, uncovered, until golden brown. Try to keep the foil as neat as possible so that it looks presentable and not all torn and scrunched up when brought to the table.
10. When the potatoes and chicken are brown, rewrap by twisting the foil in the middle (be careful not to burn yourself).
11. Serve with rice or couscous.

SERVES 6

fall-off-the-bone LAMB SHANKS AND ALMOND COUSCOUS

If you are a lamb fan this will really get your mouth watering. It is a fusion of soft couscous, crispy almonds and succulent meat.

freshly ground black pepper to taste

4 lamb shanks (ask your butcher to knick each one in two places)

1 Tbsp cake flour

little oil for frying

SAUCE

1 large onion, peeled and chopped

1 x 410 g can chopped peeled tomatoes

3 celery sticks, chopped

4 cloves garlic, finely chopped

2 cups red wine or chicken stock

handful of fresh origanum, chopped

1 tsp sugar

¼ tsp ground cinnamon

1 tsp grated lemon zest

4 sprigs of rosemary, needles removed

35 g fresh parsley, chopped

½ tsp salt

ALMOND COUSCOUS

2 cups couscous

¼ cup extra-virgin olive oil

3 sprigs of fresh mint, chopped

2 cups chicken stock

100 g flaked almonds

3 sprigs of fresh parsley, chopped

1. Grind black pepper over the lamb shanks, then dust with the flour.
2. Heat the oil in a frying pan and brown the shanks.
3. While browning, place all the sauce ingredients in a food processor and blend until smooth.
4. Remove the shanks from the pan and place in a roasting dish.
5. Preheat the oven to 160 °C.
6. Pour the sauce into the same frying pan that you used to brown the shanks and bring to the boil. Remove from the heat and pour over the shanks. Cover the dish with foil or a lid.
7. Roast in the oven for 1½ hours, covered.
8. Uncover and roast for a further 1½ hours, basting every 30 minutes or so. If the shanks aren't getting brown and glazed, turn up the heat a little, but don't let them dry out. If you feel they are getting too dry, replace the lid or foil.
9. To make the almond couscous, mix the couscous with the olive oil and mint in a large bowl. Bring the chicken stock to the boil in a small saucepan and pour over the couscous. Cover and allow to stand for 20 minutes, undisturbed. While the couscous is standing, toast the almonds in the oven until golden brown. Using a large fork, fluff up the couscous and sprinkle with the parsley and toasted almonds before serving with the lamb shanks.

SERVES 8

TRI-CORNERED PASTA PILLOWS with rose sauce

The first part of this recipe is a basic kreplach recipe (who said the Italians invented ravioli?), so on Yom Kippur, to start the fast, this is the recipe I would use for my kreplach soup. Kreplach can be made in advance and frozen. In fact, if you're going to make up a batch, double up and freeze a tray. If you want to use these kreplach in chicken soup, then follow the recipe up until step 11 in the method.

KREPLACH DOUGH
2 extra-large eggs
2 Tbsp cold water
2 cups cake flour
1 tsp salt

MEAT FILLING
little oil for frying
250 g mince
1 onion, peeled and finely grated
¾ cup cold water
salt and pepper to taste

ROSE SAUCE
1 x 410 g can chopped peeled tomatoes
handful of fresh basil leaves, chopped
1 heaped tsp sugar
3 cloves garlic, crushed
1 cup non-dairy creamer (I use Orley Whip™ Cook 'n Crème)
1 Tbsp cornflour
1 fresh chilli, chopped (optional)

1. In a large mixing bowl, beat the eggs and water for about 2 minutes.
2. Add the flour, a ¼ cup at a time, and the salt and continue to mix until well blended.
3. Knead to form a soft, smooth dough. Place the dough in a bowl, cover with cling film and leave to relax while you make the meat filling.
4. Heat the oil in a frying pan and fry the mince and onion, stirring continuously, until all the mince has browned.
5. Add ½ cup of the water, season with salt and pepper, reduce the heat and simmer for about 10 minutes until most of the moisture has evaporated.
6. Remove from the heat, allow to cool slightly and refrigerate for a while.
7. In the meantime, roll out the dough on a floured surface. Roll it out very thinly, but not quite paper-thin. Almost!
8. Cut into 5 x 5 cm squares – you could get anything from 20–25 squares.
9. Place a heaped teaspoon of the cooled mince in the middle of each square, dip your finger in the remaining water (left over from the mince mixture) and run it around the edges of the square.
10. Fold into a triangle and press down the edges to seal. Trim and neaten if you find the edges a little too long for the pocket of meat.
11. You can freeze the kreplach at this point in a single layer on a flat, lightly floured tray. Once frozen, transfer to a Ziploc™ bag. Defrost before cooking.
12. To cook, place 2 litres of salted water in a pot and bring to the boil.
13. Once boiling, add 10–12 kreplach at a time and cook for 10–15 minutes. Remove with a slotted spoon and carefully place in a rectangular glass dish.
14. To make the sauce, place all the ingredients in a bowl and mix well.
15. Transfer to a saucepan and bring to the boil over a medium to high heat.
16. Once boiling, remove from the heat and transfer the sauce to a food processor or use a hand blender to blend until smooth.
17. Reheat when ready to serve.
18. Reheat the kreplach in boiling water, removing with a slotted spoon. Plate 3–4 per person, spoon the sauce over the kreplach and serve immediately. Decorate with fresh basil leaves. Alternatively, pour the sauce over the kreplach and reheat in the microwave (1 minute per serving) or place all the kreplach with the sauce in a large ovenproof dish and bake in the oven at 190 °C for 15–20 minutes until the sauce starts to bubble.

MAKES 20–25

MOROCCAN chicken balls À LA MORDECHAI

Have you ever wondered what to do with that poor old chicken that's sat in your chicken stockpot for five hours delivering the best taste to your chicken soup ever? Well, you can't 'gooi it out', as we say in South Africa, so here's what to do with it. These chicken balls are great served cold for Shabbat lunch with hummus and pitas. Promise me you won't leave out the fresh herbs, because their flavour will take an ordinary meatball to a new majestic level, fit to be served in any palace!

1 whole boiled chicken (this can be substituted with any leftover cooked beef or lamb – 500–750 g)
1 onion, peeled and finely chopped
1 bunch of fresh coriander, finely chopped
2 Tbsp finely chopped fresh parsley
handful of fresh mint leaves, finely chopped
1 Tbsp chilli sauce (see page 25) (optional)
1 x 90 g envelope falafel mix
½–¾ cup cold water
2 eggs, lightly beaten
½–¾ cup cornflake crumbs
salt and pepper to taste
oil for frying

1. Remove all the skin and bones from the chicken, ensuring that there are no little bones left in the meat.
2. Mince the chicken through a mincer or pulse it a few times in a food processor. Place the chicken in a large bowl.
3. Add the remaining ingredients (except the oil) and mix until well combined.
4. Using your hands, roll the mixture into falafel-sized balls.
5. You can freeze them at this point, individually, on a tray. Once frozen, transfer them to a plastic bag for easier storage in the freezer. Simply defrost before deep-frying.
6. Half-fill a frying pan with oil. When hot, drop the chicken balls into the pan and fry until dark brown.
7. Serve warm or cold, piled on a plate surrounded by fresh bread and side dishes of hummus and tahini.
8. Alternatively, cut pitas into quarters and fill with a spoon of hummus, a spoon of tahini and a chicken ball or two. They won't remain on the serving platter for long!

MAKES 20–25

PERSIAN carpet rides

As a Bat Mitzvah present, my grandfather Natie took me to Israel, Persia and the Far East. I could understand going to Israel, but why Persia? Well, he had his reasons, because it was there that he bought me a Persian carpet and said, 'This is for you, my darling, a wedding present – who knows if I'll be around then, but as long as I'm here now, let's enjoy this moment.' Today the carpet hangs on a wall in my lounge. Was he at my wedding? Of course he was; maybe not in person, but he would have brought heaven down to earth to be there even if he took a magic carpet ride!

500 g beef mince
1 medium onion, peeled and grated
2 cloves garlic, crushed
1 tsp ground cumin
1 cup cooked rice
salt and pepper to taste
pinch of cayenne pepper
400 g baby-leaf spinach
little oil for frying
juice of 1 lemon
1 tsp sugar
¾ cup tomato juice

1. Combine the mince, onion, garlic, cumin, rice, salt, pepper and cayenne pepper in a large bowl and mix until well combined. Roll teaspoons of the mixture into oblong balls.
2. Boil up a pot of water and dip the spinach leaves into it to soften them. They should take about 1 minute to soften. Plunge them immediately into cold water, then drain well.
3. On a flat surface, position two or three spinach leaves so that they are overlapping each other. Place an oblong-shaped mince ball on the leaves, pull the leaves up around the meat and roll up as you would a Swiss roll.
4. Repeat until all the mince balls are used up.
5. Heat the oil in a frying pan and pack the spinach rolls tightly into it.
6. Combine the lemon juice, sugar and tomato juice in a bowl and mix well.
7. Once the spinach rolls start to crackle a little in the oil, pour over the tomato sauce.
8. Bring to the boil and then reduce the heat.
9. Place a plate on top of the spinach rolls to prevent them from floating and simmer for about 45 minutes.
10. Don't let all the juice reduce – the spinach rolls should be nicely glazed, but not swimming in sauce.
11. Serve on a bed of couscous or on their own as a side dish.

MAKES 25–30

To-crown-it-all peaches

to-crown-it-all PEACHES

After eating all those hamantaschen followed by a Seuda, we crown it all with a twist in the tale. This is a deceiving dessert that fits in well with the Purim theme: what you see is not what you get. But no mask can hide the wonderful and delicious taste sensation you are about to experience!

2 x 825 g cans peach halves in syrup
2 Tbsp white wine vinegar
4 cinnamon sticks
2 x 4 cm pieces ginger, peeled and sliced into rounds
1 fresh red chilli, halved and deseeded or 1 tsp dried chilli flakes
1 tsp coarse koshering salt
1 tsp whole black peppercorns
6 whole cloves

1. Place all the ingredients in a saucepan and bring to the boil. Immediately turn off the heat, place a lid on top and allow to cool.
2. Transfer to a glass bowl and refrigerate.
3. Serve chilled with vanilla ice cream.

SERVES 8–10

poppy seed MUFFINS

I agree that there's nothing nicer than making your own hamantaschen, but let's be realistic: there is so much to do on Purim that I don't mind leaving the hamantaschen to the bakeries. However, poppy seed muffins are a breeze to make and can be made the day before and eaten for breakfast! Okay, so they're not three cornered, but they're round to represent Queen Esther's crown and that's good enough for me!

1 x 800 g box of your favourite vanilla cake mix
⅓ cup poppy seeds
1 heaped tsp finely grated lemon rind

ICING
2 cups sifted icing sugar
2 Tbsp non-dairy margarine
juice of 1 lemon

1. Preheat the oven according to the instructions on the cake-mix box.
2. Make up the cake mix as per the instructions on the box. Instead of using milk, use either soy milk, coconut milk or water. Add the poppy seeds and lemon rind and mix until well combined.
3. Spoon the mixture into large paper cookie cups (three-quarters of the way up the sides) and set in muffin trays.
4. Bake as per the instructions on the cake-mix box.
5. Once baked, remove from the oven and allow to cool while you make the icing.
6. To make the icing, combine all the ingredients in a bowl and mix well. If the icing is too firm, add one tablespoon at a time of water until the desired consistency is reached. Ice the cooled cupcakes and sprinkle with poppy seeds.

MAKES 18

INDEX

*Page numbers in **bold** indicate photographs.*

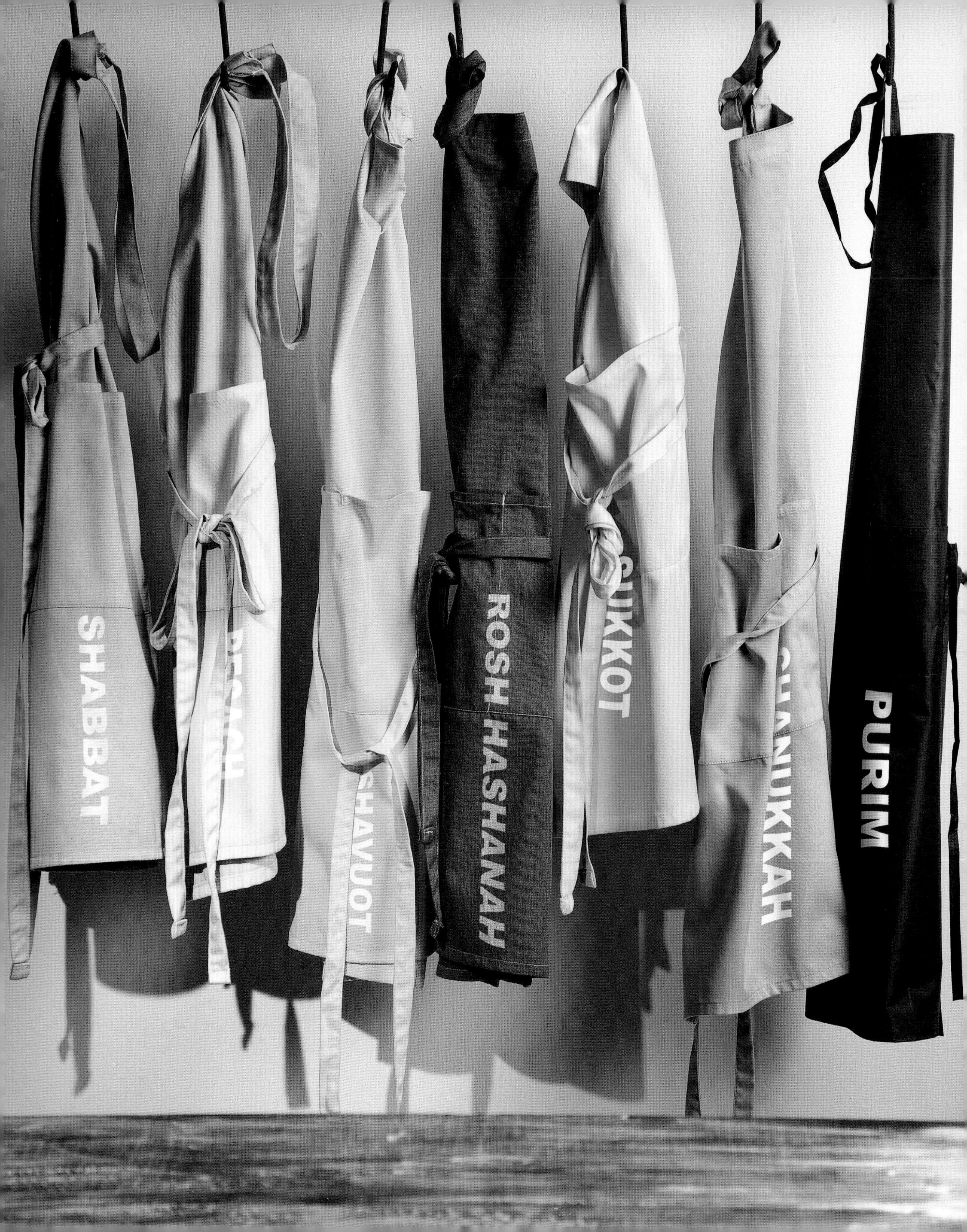
SHABBAT
SHAVUOT
ROSH HASHANAH
SUKKOT
PURIM